25 SKI TOURS IN THE GREEN MOUNTAINS

7860615

Hist 917.43044 F711t
Ford, Sally
25 ski tours in the Green
 Mountains $4.95

MAIN LIBRARY

Memphis and Shelby
County Public Library and
Information Center

For the Residents
of
Memphis and Shelby County

DISCARD

Abandoned house on the Cram Hill Loop (see Tour 19)

25 SKI TOURS IN THE GREEN MOUNTAINS

SALLY AND DANIEL FORD

 New Hampshire Publishing Company   Somersworth

An invitation to the reader:

If you find that your favorite trail has not been included,
or that a trailhead has been moved or landmarks changed,
please write:

Editor, 25 Ski Tours
New Hampshire Publishing Company
P.O. Box 70
Somersworth, New Hampshire 03878

Library of Congress Catalog Card Number 78-56097
International Standard Book Number 0-912274-93-X

© 1978 by Sally and Daniel Ford. All rights reserved.

Printed in the United States of America

Photographs by the authors
Design by David Ford

To Rudi Mattesich,
president of the Ski Touring Council,
we fondly dedicate this book

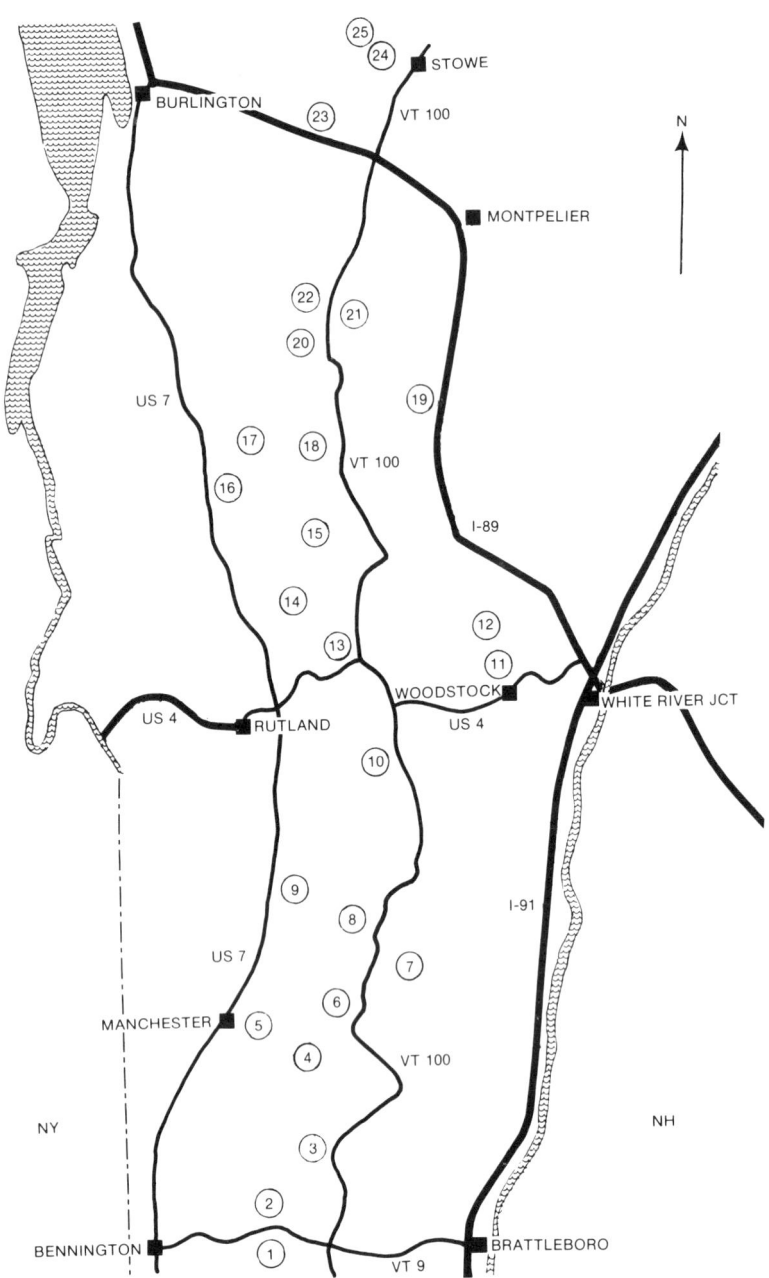

Contents

Introduction 9

1. Beaver Lodge Trail 15
2. Little Pond 19
3. Country Club Loop 23
4. Stratton Pond 27
5. Prospect Rock 31
6. Mill Brook Trail 35
7. Cobble Hill Loop 39
8. Utley Brook Trail 43
9. Mount Tabor Road 49
10. Northam Shelter 53
11. Mount Tom 57
12. Webster Hill 62
13. Gifford Woods 68
14. Reservoir Loop 72
15. Chittenden Brook 76
16. Silver Lake 81
17. Frost Farm Loop 87
18. Texas Falls 91
19. Cram Hill Loop 95
20. Austin Brook 101
21. Ole's Loop 105
22. Tucker Hill 110
23. Bolton Lodge 115
24. Trapp Cabin Loop 119
25. Smuggler's Notch 123

Introduction

Vermont and the Green Mountains are almost synonymous. In fact, Vermont *means* "green mountain" in French, if you allow for the uncertainties of eighteenth-century spelling. North and south, the mountains reach all the way from Massachusetts to the Canada line. East and west they are more variable, sometimes extending from border to border and sometimes confined to one central ridge, but always a barrier to be reckoned with. There's a lot of skiing in those mountains. (A lot of driving, too. "You can't get there from here" is a joke attributed to various New England states, but which applies especially to Vermont, especially when winter has closed some of the upland connector roads.) Choosing Vermont for the skiing is a bit like choosing London for the theater—it's a great idea, but exactly where do you start?

This book is our answer. To simplify matters, and to keep you from spending most of your time on the road, we took the liberty of squaring off the Green Mountains here and there. Northbound, we drew the line at Smuggler's Notch. Anything beyond that point must wait for a book about skiing the Northeast Kingdom, which is as different from the rest of Vermont as Vermont is different from the rest of New England. East and west, we sometimes strayed from the main range of mountains. For example, we figured that skiers who toured Vermont without scheduling at least one visit to the Woodstock area were cheating themselves. So we put it in, knowing full well that not even the local chamber of commerce would

Introduction

claim Woodstock as a Green Mountain town. (You can see the Green Mountains from there, as the local touring director was quick to point out.)

What we ended with was a territory bounded by Bennington and Brattleboro in the south, Burlington and Barre in the north. That's still a considerable stretch of mountains, foothills, and river valleys, so we made a further decision to cluster our ski tours whenever we could. If you're lodging in West Dover, for example, you'll find not one but half a dozen tours within an easy drive, and one of them will almost certainly suit your skiing ability and your thirst for adventure.

While we limited ourselves to backcountry trails whenever possible, a number of our choices turned out to be connected with commercial touring centers. There are two reasons for this. In the first place, Vermont was an early and enthusiastic recruit to the cross-country revolution: there are more touring centers here than in any other New England state. Since few touring centers own land enough to satisfy the ambitious skier, most have spread themselves onto public or private land nearby. Thus what would have been a wilderness trail in another state often turned out to be a groomed track in Vermont.

The second reason for including so many touring centers is that, even in one year, cross-country skiing has registered an astonishing growth. Not long ago, it was a rare landowner who objected to strangers passing through. As the number of strangers increased, however, the signs began to go up: no hunting, no snowmobiling, and finally no anything. The sad fact is that skiers have become a bit of a pest. For some reason, people will trespass on snow where they wouldn't dream of intruding in the summer months, and often enough they are accom-

Introduction

panied by large dogs with uncertain manners. Ski touring, like hunting and snowmobiling, has thus become a sport subject to regulation and sometimes prohibition. Accordingly, we have tried to guide you to places where you will be greeted kindly. If that means paying two dollars for a trail fee, well, that's the price you must pay for living in the second half of the twentieth century, when the good life has suddenly become a very popular life indeed.

Our tours are arranged from south to north. We assume that you have a good road map (the official Vermont state map is the best, and widely available). By comparing this map with the sketch which faces the table of contents, you should find several tours within driving distance of where you are or where you plan to be, and very

A stuffed animal makes a good trail companion for a youngster

Introduction

likely they will follow one another in the book. *Please read the trail descriptions in advance.* Especially study the three items which introduce the text:

Distance. In every case the distance is calculated in miles from start to finish. (Sometimes the trailhead may be a few hundred yards from the parking area, requiring you to walk or ski that much extra, but this fact will be mentioned in the text.) These measurements are the best we could obtain, relying on the U.S. Geological Survey, local opinion, and our own experience in skiing the trail. Unless you follow a vigorous and ski-oriented exercise program, you should begin with the shorter tours. Five miles is about right for the average recreational skier. (You'll find that you can go much farther on a groomed track, while a foot of newfallen snow can make even one mile seem like a journey to the ends of the earth.) Later in the season, when the days are longer and your muscles have hardened, you will be able to enjoy the eight- or ten-mile treks.

Difficulty. We call ourselves intermediate skiers, and we assume that if we can ski a trail with pleasure, most people can do likewise. Thus we rate each tour according to the difficulty we experienced in traveling it—slight, moderate, or considerable—after making due allowance for the weather and the condition of the track. After skiing one or two of these trails, you'll discover how your step-turn compares with ours. If you find yourself sweating on trails we've rated "moderate," then please do not attempt the three tours where the difficulty is "considerable." They are Prospect Rock (#5), Utley Brook Trail (#8), and Cram Hill Loop (#19).

Introduction

Map. Personally, we never go into the backcountry without a contour map, which in Vermont generally means a topographical sheet from the U.S. Geological Survey. (The Green Mountain National Forest also publishes topographical sheets, and often these are more current, but they are not so widely available.) Such maps are both a safety measure and a means of increasing our enjoyment of the countryside. However, we know that many skiers just won't go to the trouble and expense of obtaining these sheets, so if there's a reasonable alternative we list it here. Usually it's a ski-touring map published by a local club or touring center; such maps are identified by the letters "XC" before the title, and in the text you'll learn where to obtain them. In several cases only the USGS sheet will do. These are available by mail and sometimes at bookstores and ski shops in the vicinity.

We have not attempted to estimate the time you should allot to a tour. Unless we're skiing in a prepared track, we find that two miles an hour is a pace that gives us plenty of scope for sightseeing and picnicking, and which always brings us home in good season. Thus we took six hours on the Utley Brook Trail, five hours on the Cram Hill Loop. Often we're passed by the hard chargers who look upon skiing as exercise rather than recreation; less often we find ourselves passing people who view it as pure relaxation. Skiers differ, and so does their speed over the snow. And the same skier, on the same trail, may discover that yesterday's time must be doubled to allow for today's snow conditions. Finally, there's a vast difference between December and March in northern New England. Early in the season, the shadows are long by two o'clock in the afternoon; by three, the glory has left the day. We truly believe that there's no such thing as an afternoon tour in the Green Mountains of Vermont.

Introduction

Start early, take a picnic lunch, and you'll double both your pleasure and your margin of safety.

* * *

We are more than usually indebted to the people who helped us do the field work for this book. They included Rudi Mattesich, Serena and Phil Paine, Thom Bailey, Richard M. Brett, Ned Gillette, John Wiggin, John Eckhardt, Darrell M. Frogness, Wolfgang F. Schumann, John Shuell, Dory Ryan, Tony Clark, Clyde Smith, Dorothy Evans, Dorothy Perry, Art Norton, Anne Mausolff, Max Petersen, John Tidd, Zeke Church, Paul M. Kihlmire, Jr., Raymond J. Harwood, John Michael White, Don Cochrane, Ole Mosesen, Stan Allaben, and some whose names we failed to catch, including the six who helped us start our car on a twenty-below morning in Middlebury Gap.

1 Beaver Lodge Trail

To pond and return: 6½ miles

Difficulty: moderate

Map: XC Bennington

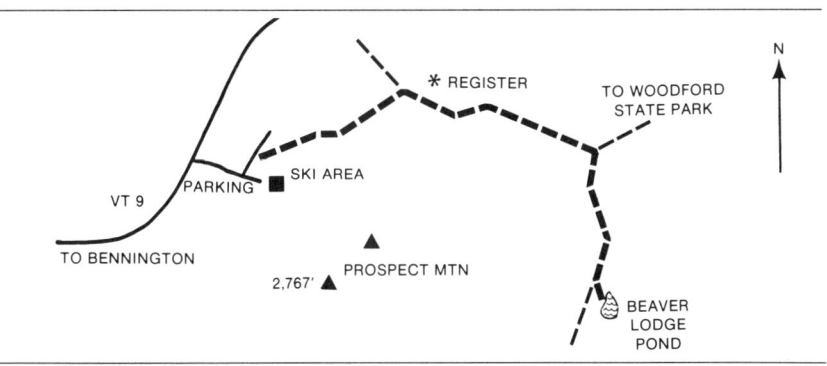

When you are admiring the geography of Vermont, do not overlook the role played by the lowly beaver, who with sharp teeth and boundless energy can transform a swamp into a sparkling pond—and eventually into meadowland. A large beaver works can be found near Prospect Mountain, east of Bennington, together with a particularly fine beaver lodge. The trail to it was cut and marked (and is regularly patrolled) by the Bennington Nordic Ski Patrol. It is shown on a map-brochure called "Tracks in the Snow," sold at local ski shops and by the Chamber of Commerce; the cost at this writing is less than $1. By all means pick up a copy. The map shows hundreds of miles of ski, snowshoe, and snowmobile

1   Beaver Lodge Trail

trails in this southwestern corner of Vermont, together with helpful information on backcountry travel.

Drive to Prospect Mountain ski area, 8 miles east of Bennington on VT 9, and leave your car in the outer parking lot. Walk across the bridge toward the lifts and warming hut, but before reaching them turn left on a plowed road. The trail begins in about 200 yards, marked by an orange sign and streamers. Ski to the right and uphill on an old road, which soon takes you into a field; keep to the right and pick up the trail on the other side. The course is generally northeast through the evergreens, with one sharp turn to the right. (There is a sign here: 2½ miles to Woodford State Park. The left fork is an unmarked road leading back toward the highway.) The trail then crosses a brook and follows it uphill on a more easterly course, through a hardwood grove and into the evergreens again.

After a slight downhill, the trail meets another old road and again turns sharply to the right and uphill. The course here is almost due south. After a straight and level stretch, you'll come to a register box provided by the Bennington Nordic Ski Patrol, about 1¼ miles from the start. This is followed by another downhill, past a small pond on the right, and then a sign for the Green Mountain National Forest. Soon thereafter you'll come to a trail junction, about 2 miles from the start. The left fork will take you in ½ mile to Woodford State Park and the Allis Reservoir. (The sign promises ¼ mile, but that's only to the end of the ski trail and the beginning of the "blue trail" around the reservoir. The latter is skiable, but just barely.)

Turning right (south) for Beaver Lodge Pond, the trail takes you downhill, then up. It was a rather scrubby path

1 Beaver Lodge Trail

when we passed through, but on the return leg we met two ski patrollers with saws and clippers, so you will probably find it trimmer than we did. After a steep uphill climb you come to the height-of-land, with views northward to Castle Meadows and Stratton Mountain. From here it is a gradual descent to the beaver pond, 3¼ miles from the start. The old road passes to the right of the pond; follow the orange streamers to the shore or just bushwhack through. The beaver lodge—about five feet tall and ten feet in diameter—is on the uppermost of several dammed areas, two or three acres in extent. Drowned trees project from the ice, while the living trees on the shore may show the teeth marks of the industrious

Food, warmth, and safety are provided by the beaver lodge

1   Beaver Lodge Trail

beaver. In the springtime you may actually find them at work, but if it is deep winter, they'll be snug in their lodge, insulated by brush and snow from the outside temperatures, and protected by their underwater entrance from you and all other intruders. Food—in the form of tender branches—is also hoarded under the ice.

Ski back the way you came. There is a nice downhill run on the beaver-lodge spur, and another as you approach Prospect Mountain ski area. Don't forget to sign in when you pass the register box, which is examined on a regular basis by the Nordic Ski Patrol. Mostly the messages are just friendly chatter, but sometimes this information can be useful in finding a skier who is overdue.

2 Little Pond

To pond and
return: 5 miles

Difficulty:
slight

Map: XC
Bennington

Maybe it was the sunshine after four gray days, or the overnight fall of snow, or the January air with the tart flavor of an old-fashioned apple, but we remember this tour as one of the prettiest we've ever taken. Little Pond, located about 10 miles east of Bennington, is tucked back in the woods but easily reached by an old access road that the Forest Service keeps clear for purposes of fire control, fish and game husbandry, and recreation. This is a popular route for all manner of winter travelers, but never to the point where they jostle one another. We visited Little Pond on a Sunday; we saw snowmobile and ski tracks from the day before, and we met a pair of snowshoers back at the highway. Otherwise we had the entire lovely trail to ourselves.

The handiest map for this trip is "Tracks in the Snow," published by the Bennington Nordic Ski Patrol (see Tour 1), although the access road is also shown on the USGS Woodford sheet. To find Little Pond, look first for Big Pond, a lake community just off VT 9 between Prospect Mountain ski area and Woodford State Park. The trailhead is at the height-of-land as you drive east, ½ mile beyond Big Pond. There's a large white house on the north side of the highway, then a pull-off where the plows

2 Little Pond

have made room for a dozen cars by the side of the road. A power line crosses the highway at this point and enters the woods on the same right-of-way that you will use. Park parallel to the highway and climb the embankment; then ski into the woods and almost immediately turn left. This maneuver puts you behind the white house and onto the Little Pond access road, which itself has no parking area. Turn right (north) into a cleared roadway. It climbs steadily for a time, though not too steeply for well-waxed skis; then it levels off, passes the wreckage of an old cottage, and crosses an east-west transmission line, ½ mile from the start.

After the transmission line, Little Pond road climbs more gently and enters a field, where it follows a stone wall and a neat file of spruce trees to another cottage, this one in far better condition and set off by some gigantic Christmas-tree firs. To the south there is a fine view of Prospect Mountain. The road now reenters the woods, with a plantation of red pines on the right, laid out in a perfect checkerboard grid.

After a time the road levels off and even descends a bit, through woods that are now open and mostly deciduous. This is the ridge of Hagar Hill, with twin humps like a Bactrian camel. The road goes up and down, through a plantation of spruce and red pine, and again into the hardwood forest. Finally another road comes in from the left, and the trail—it does seem to be more of a trail now and less of an access road—turns to the right and rather steeply downhill. Novice skiers should take care, especially if a snowmobile has left its narrow track in the middle of the trail. The pond is at the bottom of the slope. It is a perfect gem, seemingly a hundred miles from the nearest road instead of the 2½ miles you have actually

◀ Red pine plantation on the trail to Little Pond

2   Little Pond

traveled. Cupped by higher ground on all sides, it offers a sheltered spot for your picnic.

A strong party could bushwhack due east to Forest Road 272, which leads back to the highway at a point about ½ mile beyond where you left your car. The loop entails about 6 miles of skiing. However, the bushwhack cuts through decidedly rough country, and you should be equipped with both the Nordic Ski Patrol map (which shows FR 272) and the USGS sheet (which doesn't) before attempting this variant. You will also need a compass and the ability to use it. Novice and intermediate skiers will prefer to return the way they arrived. The southern half of Little Pond access road is a delightful downhill run, never too steep for pleasurable skiing, and scarcely leveling off for the better part of a mile.

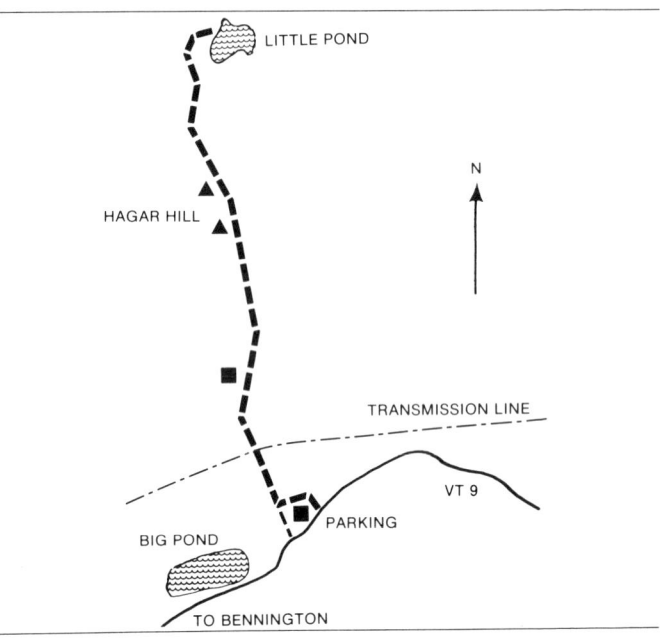

3 Country Club Loop

Around the loop: 5 miles

Difficulty: mostly slight

Map: XC Mt. Snow

If you prefer luncheon to picnics in the snow—or a hot toddy to tea from a thermos—this is the tour for you. Each winter the Mount Snow Country Club transforms itself into the Mount Snow Ski Touring Center. The fairways become practice loops, the pro shop becomes a ski shop, and the tavern-restaurant adds a Franklin stove to its decor. Unlike most golf-course touring centers, however, Mount Snow boasts a backcountry loop five miles around. It's a perfect trip for a blustery winter day. You'll be in the woods for much of the distance, the trail is groomed so the miles go quickly, and there's a crackling fire awaiting your return.

To find it, take Country Club Road on the west side of VT 100, between West Dover village and the access road to Mount Snow ski area. A motel, steak house, and other enterprises are clustered at the intersection. Country Club Road twists and climbs and finally makes a 90° turn to the left. The touring center and ample parking are on the right just after the turn. At this writing the trail fee is $2, map included. While you are in the touring center (shop and waxing room below, food and drink above) you might ask somebody to show you the beginning of the "Long Trail," as it is somewhat confusingly called.

3 Country Club Loop

Because the trail system utilizes the fairways, and because skiers wander here and there as the fancy takes them, the formal trails are not always easy to locate.

To start, as they say in the army, you want to make a left oblique from the touring center. That is, ski southeast, leaving the building behind you and to your right. Go under the power line which leads to the Mount Snow airport, whose access road is unplowed but visible because of the trees that line it. The trail begins here, marked by a blue sign and a blue diamond. Follow the prepared track uphill to the south, keeping fairly close to the airport road. You'll pass a hangar (on your right) and a gazebo (on your left) before entering the woods about 1 mile from the start. You'll have no further difficulty with pathfinding. The trail is wide and marked at frequent intervals by blue diamonds bearing the initials "CC."

The trail meanders for a time through the hardwoods, then turns south at a steep downhill that is preceded by a caution sign. Believe the sign! For 100 feet or so, the "Long Trail" is truly sporty, with a double downhill turn and not much room to ponder. Don't turn back on that account, however. It's the only worrisome spot. After a pleasant woodland stretch, the trail swings around to the right and joins a logging road, then turns south again through the woods. About 2 miles from the start, a cut-off provides the shortest return to the touring center, while the "Long Trail" picks up another road westward-bound.

Soon it cuts into yet another road and bears north for the first time. The terrain is gently downhill now, and the trail meanders for a considerable distance before turning sharp right again, about 3½ miles from the start. Straight ahead at this turning, you can see the trails of Haystack

3   Country Club Loop

Mountain ski area. (In that direction a strong party can ski out to the Handle Road and thus to the Hermitage Inn, which has its own touring network. The 1-mile link is not always broken out, however.) Continuing north on the "Long Trail," you'll ski through the woods for another ½ mile before emerging on the fairways. From here it's a loopy 1-mile track back to the touring center, the exact route being at the whim of the snowmobile operator who sets the track. He appears to have a sense of humor, or at least a sense of adventure, never taking the short distance when a longer one will do, and never going around a hill if he can manage to go over it.

Incidentally, this loop is seven miles according to local

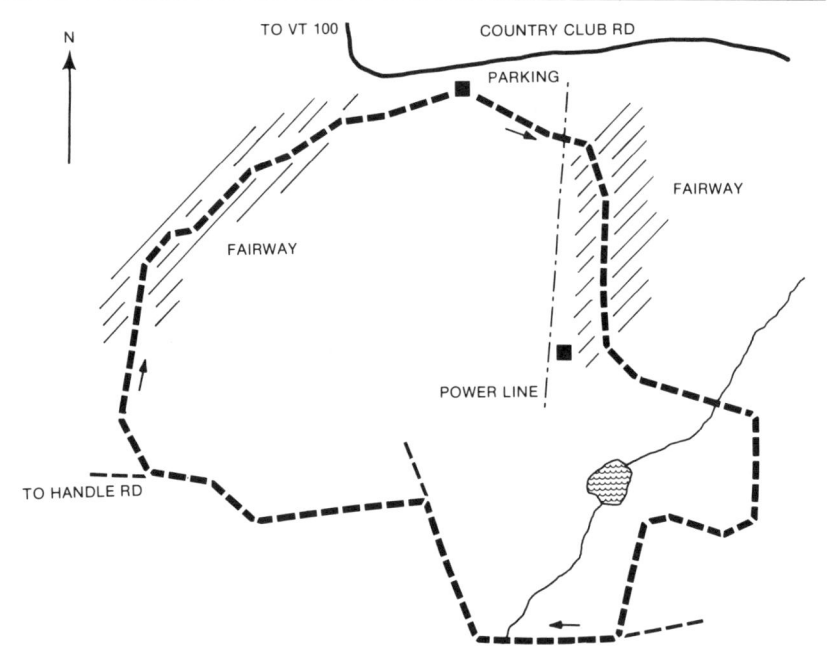

3   Country Club Loop

estimates. Perhaps so, but we believe the shorter distance is more accurate, whether judged by muscle fatigue or the USGS Wilmington sheet.

Family conference on the Country Club Loop

4 Stratton Pond

To pond and
return: 6 miles

Difficulty:
moderate

Map: XC
Stratton

Stratton Pond is the largest and most popular body of water on the Long Trail, and upwards of 2,000 people spend a night here every summer. In winter it's much less crowded. Still, quite a few skiers and snowshoers do make the trek, using the pond's overnight shelters as convenient places for a picnic.

Although not a maintained trail, the route to Stratton Pond from the east has been adopted by the local touring center, whose staff clears the downed timber from time to time and provides skiers a trail map and advice without charge. The touring center is on the access road to Stratton Mountain ski area, off VT 30 a few miles east of Manchester. It's a handsome facility with a tavern, food service, and fireplace in addition to the usual amenities. Inquire here about the current attitude toward parking at the end of North Brookwood Road. In the past, most Stratton Pond skiers have begun the trek from the turnaround, leaving their cars at a sign forbidding them to do so. If no storm is threatening, and if the town fathers haven't hardened their attitude since we made the tour, you might as well do the same. Pick up North Brookwood on your right as you drive toward the moun-

Stratton Pond

tain, and follow it to its end at the turnaround between two seasonal homes. Here Stratton Pond Trail enters the trees and immediately turns to the right (west), its route marked with orange diamonds. A few yards to the south, you'll be able to hear and perhaps see the downhill skiers on a novice slope known as Wanderer.

Bigelow Shelter offers a lunch break under cover

4 Stratton Pond

(If you are advised not to leave your car on North Brookwood, drive to the downhill ski area and begin the tour from there. Walk to the right of the base lodge and chairlifts, and ski uphill on Wanderer. Keep well to the right. The trail divides twice; bear right each time, leaving the downhill slope just after you pass the last of the trailside houses, abreast of the turnaround on North Brookwood. This variation adds ¾ mile to the distances noted below, and 1½ miles to the trip overall. The climb on Wanderer—and the descent on your way home—is too difficult for novice tour-skiers.)

The Stratton Pond Trail sets off westward through the scrub, trending downhill along an old road now growing to brambles. It soon crosses a brook, then turns due west, descending steadily and sometimes steeply. Finally there is a long, gentle downhill run to a pond. Here the trail levels off, crosses another brook, and comes to a fine stand of yellow birch where a side-trail comes in from the right. Then you cross a field, formerly an apple orchard. On the far side the trail bears off to the northwest and uphill (there are some surveyor's marks on the trees) along the old road.

After crossing a knoll, the trail drops down to the south shore of Stratton Pond at a summer tenting area. By skirting the shore you'll come to the intersection with the Long Trail (Massachusetts is 31 miles to your left; Canada is 231 miles straight on). Bigelow Shelter stands at the shoreline just beyond, about 3 miles from the start. It tilts rather dramatically toward the pond, despite having been rebuilt a few years ago. There are two other shelters in the area: Vondell to the west and Stratton View on the north shore. (This last, as its name promises, has an outlook on the mountain to the southeast.) Returning, you'll be pleasantly surprised to find that the hills seem

4   Stratton Pond

much less steep than they did on the outward journey, so that you'll end with the best of both worlds: a downhill run that in the reverse direction requires very few acrobatics to ascend. Properly waxed, you can walk right up the worst of them.

Exercise great care if your return route takes you down Wanderer. You'll find yourself in the company of downhill skiers traveling very fast indeed, often without matching skill.

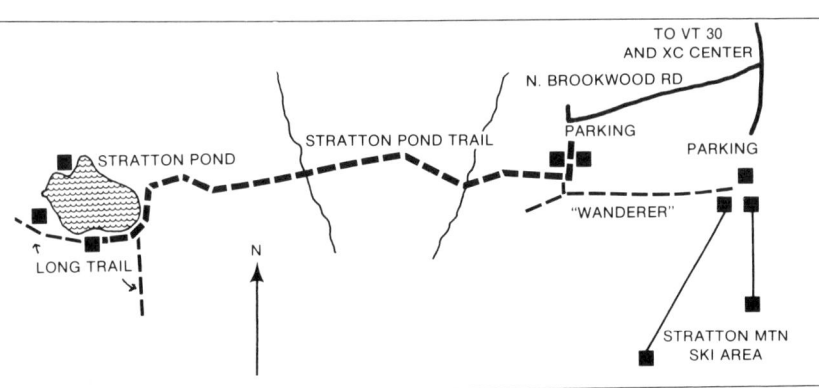

5 Prospect Rock

To outlook
and return:
4 miles

Difficulty:
considerable

Map: USGS
Manchester

The Lye Brook Wilderness contains more than 14,000 acres of primitive woodland, protected by Congressional decree from any activity more destructive than foot travel. To enter this preserve you must have a permit from the U.S. Forest Service. Strictly speaking, the trail to Prospect Rock merely skirts the wilderness area, but if you want to explore you should first schedule a stop at the Forest Service office in Manchester Center (on US 7 just north of its junction with VT 30). At the same time you can obtain a copy of the Green Mountain National Forest map of Lye Brook; while not as legible as the USGS sheet, it does show the entire wilderness area.

Thus equipped, drive to Manchester Depot on VT 30 and VT 11. Just beyond, you'll come upon a motel, a restaurant, and a double road intersection; the side streets are labeled East Manchester Road and Rootville Road. If you are the cautious type, you should leave your car in the restaurant parking lot and walk from here. Otherwise drive up the Rootville Road in an easterly direction. It's narrow and unpaved, but the town plows it for about ½ mile to the last house, an A-frame dwelling on the left. There is usually room at the end of the plowed section

5   Prospect Rock

for one or two cars—no more than that. If you hope to be one of them, obviously you must schedule this tour for a nonholiday weekday.

The Rootville Road now continues as a jeep track, which almost immediately swings to the right (south). It is steep for the most part, and heavily snowmobiled; this combination of a steep pitch and a narrow or rutted track has prompted us to label it as suitable for experts only. However, with good snow cover it should make satisfactory skiing for intermediates as well, especially those adept at waxing. About ½ mile from the end of the plowed

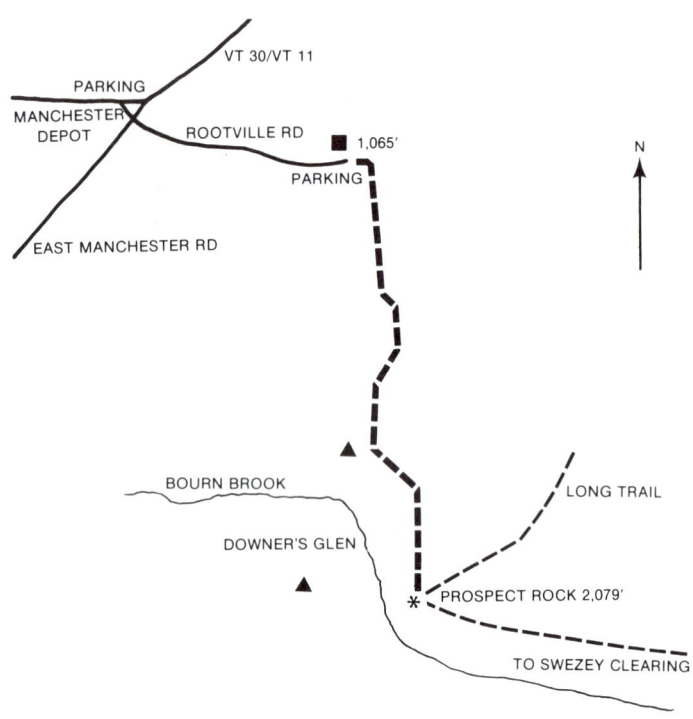

5 Prospect Rock

road, you'll come upon a sign for the Lye Brook Wilderness on the right side of the trail. You may be disappointed: it's mostly second-growth hardwoods, not the forest primeval that Longfellow sang about. However, every forest begins with scrub, and when your grandchildren pass this way they'll see a very different wilderness.

About 1½ miles from the start, the Rootville Road bears east at a red-blazed tree, then soon resumes its southward journey. The terrain is more nearly level through here, and the woods to the west have opened up, causing the snow to be drifted high in some places and scoured clean in others. To compensate, there are wild views through the birches into Downer's Glen, the gorge which carries Bourn Brook down to Manchester. This state of affairs continues almost all the way to Prospect Rock. Look for two landmarks: the white blazes of the Long Trail on your left and an automobile-sized boulder on your right. There are also some sadly stripped birches here. The side-trail to Prospect Rock is on the right, just behind the boulder and leading northwest—just about where you came from. Follow the trail about 200 feet to the outlook, which is fabulous. Downer's Glen is a V-shaped notch with the flat meadowland of Dorset Valley beyond. The village of Manchester Depot is in the foreground; Equinox Mountain is on the left and Dorset Mountain is on the right. (Remove your skis before exploring Prospect Rock, for it's a long fall into Downer's Glen.)

Weather and time permitting, you'll want to ski along the Rootville Road for about 1 mile more, to the clearing where Swezey Camp stood until recently. While generally uphill, this would be a novice tour with good snow conditions. At the clearing, the Long Trail crosses a monkey bridge and becomes a footpath in the wilder-

5   Prospect Rock

ness. Return the way you came. Use caution: the vertical drop from Prospect Rock to the plowed road is about 1,000 feet.

Take off your skis for the scramble to Prospect Rock

6 Mill Brook Trail

To dam and
return: 5 miles

Difficulty:
mostly slight

Map: XC
Woody's

Rawsonville is a highway junction a few miles below Londonderry. The main attraction is an enterprise known as Woody's Cracker Barrel, a cross between a Vermont country store and a Westchester County ski shop. Among its other amenities (there really is a barrel filled with crackers) Woody's runs a touring center complete with rentals, instruction, and a network of groomed trails. The prettiest trail, however, is located to the north along Mill Brook, which some years ago was dammed to form a considerable body of water: Gale Meadows Pond. The trail from Rawsonville is skiable by a sturdy novice, while intermediates will find miles of additional touring along the shores of the pond.

Drive to Rawsonville on VT 30 or 100. Woody's is the building with the astonishing silo, a few hundred feet east of their intersection. Because there is no parking at the trailhead, you must leave your car in Woody's commodious lot. Pick up a trail map at the store and walk back to the intersection, passing a monument to Bailey Rawson as you go. (At sixteen, young Rawson played the fife in George Washington's army of rebellion. Afterwards he traveled from town to town in New England, shoeing horses, until he came upon this spot about 1810, built a

Mill Brook Trail

sawmill, and founded the settlement that bears his name.) From the intersection, walk or ski north about 200 yards alongside VT 100. You'll cross two bridges, the first over the Winhall River, the second over Mill Brook. Just beyond the second of these, ski off to the left (west) for Mill Brook Trail.

The trail leads down to a gate which is usually left open for hikers and skiers. After another short downhill stretch, it climbs past a few seasonal cottages and enters a hem-

Mill Brook is a lively companion along the trail

6 Mill Brook Trail

lock forest. Soon afterward Mill Brook is visible on the left, a husky stream which will keep you company for most of the journey to Gale Meadows Pond. About ½ mile from the start, a power line crosses the trail. Ski straight ahead for Mill Brook Trail, which is marked at frequent intervals with red paint blazes. (Sometimes older blue blazes can also be seen.) The woods now include spruce and some magnificent white pines, over one hundred feet tall and a century old.

The trail follows Mill Brook closely for the most part, though generally on a bank high above it, until it nears Haven Hill Road. Then the trail bears off to the right on a more northerly course, crossing the road near a recently constructed house 2 miles from the start. Pick up the trail just behind a sign, directly across the road. (An unplowed road parallels the trail, a few hundred feet to the west, and many skiers follow it as the easier route.) The red blazes here were supplemented by blue streamers when we passed through. In about ½ mile of easy woods travel you'll come upon the dam site, an agreeable picnic spot.

If the hour is early and the party strong, you can continue along the east bank of the pond on the Rugg Lot Trail. Though much harder to follow, and occasionally leading through more difficult terrain, it will take you in about 1 mile to the northern shore. It leads through a hardwood forest, crosses a few small openings, and at a farmstead swings left (west) onto a logging road. We found no blazes beyond this point. However, the logging road took us uphill and down to the pond again. Caution: skiers enter these roads from all directions, so take note of your back trail in case you decide to return the way you came. Alternately, ice permitting, you can simply ski

6   Mill Brook Trail

down the pond to the dam site. Always pay close attention to your location, for Woody's trail map is rudimentary and the pond does not show on the USGS quadrangle.

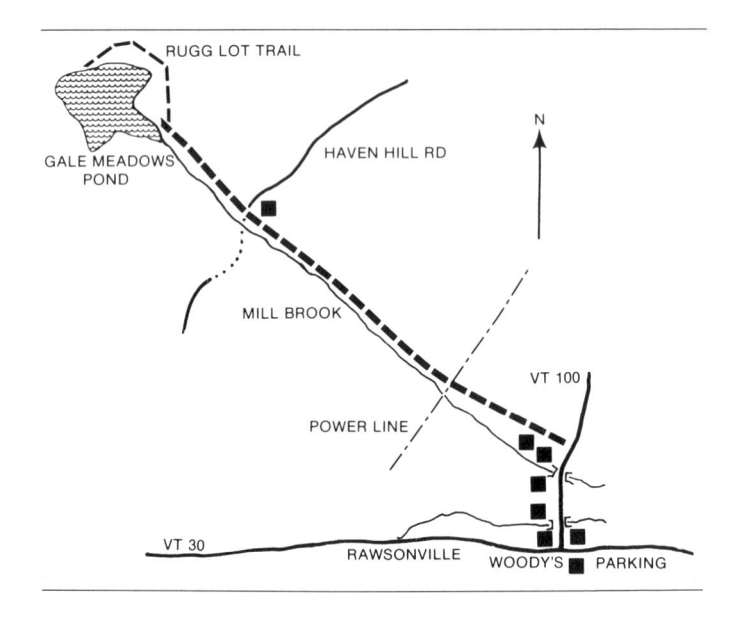

7 Cobble Hill Loop

Around the loop: 8 miles

Difficulty: moderate

Map: XC Viking

The Viking Ski Touring Center is one of the oldest around, and one of the few that is not attached to an inn or a downhill ski resort. Located just east of Londonderry, it has a parking lot that seemed huge when the Viking opened for business, but which now is cramped on weekends and holidays. Another reason for scheduling a weekday visit is the Viking's rate structure: the trail fee at this writing is $2 most days but goes up to $3 at the busy times. That sum gives you the right to ski a network of groomed trails—plus the Cobble Hill Trail, which for the most part is not groomed, and which takes you far from the touring center and through a gorgeous succession of Vermont woodlots and farmyards. The touring center is reached by following VT 11 east from Londonderry; in ¾ mile, turn left uphill on Little Pond Road, which takes you to the Viking parking lot in ½ mile.

To find the trail, ski uphill behind the touring center and take your first right onto Sugarbush Run. This leads you downhill to the beginning of Cobble Hill Trail, which is marked with blue diamonds and occasional signs throughout its distance. The trail soon crosses Boynton Road and leads through a field with young pine and

7   Cobble Hill Loop

Beginning the long circuit of Cobble Hill

7 Cobble Hill Loop

spruce and a fine view of Cobble Hill on the north. Then it enters the woods and bears left, leading you uphill and down to an intersection about 1 mile from the start. Take the right fork, which soon turns south before doubling back at the end of a downhill stretch. There's another intersection, where again you want the right-hand trail. It brings you to the plowed driveway of Cobble Hill Farm. Here, about 2 miles from the start, the groomed track ends.

Cobble Hill Trail heads north through a hardwood forest, distinctly rougher now. Eventually, however, it joins an old logging road which passes through a region of tall spruce. The trail meanders generally downhill until it crosses a brook on the ice (caution!), then another brook on a deadfall bridge. The trail then climbs toward Old Tavern Road, turning left (west) at a stone wall before reaching the right-of-way. It then crosses the driveway of a hill farm, about 4 miles from the start, where a spruce plantation makes a checkerboard upon the distant slope. The trail continues on the other side of the driveway, crossing a barbed-wire fence into a field. The route is marked by blue diamonds on nearby trees or on wands stuck in the snow. Head for a house of modern design, but double back along a stone wall before reaching it. You are now skiing almost due south, and Cobble Hill appears as a plump pyramid to the left of the direct route.

The trail enters a pine forest and turns right on a rough path, encounters a barbed-wire fence, and follows it south once more, finally crossing the fence and picking up a logging road which takes you down to Boynton Road. The trail continues on the other side of the road, taking you into a farmer's field, turning left beneath a power line, and following to a tributary of West River. (If

7 Cobble Hill Loop

the brook is open, you can cross it instead by a bridge on Boynton Road.) The trail passes close behind the farmstead, pretty much following the power line, but swinging back toward the road once you have passed the fine red barn, where the Herefords may be watching your antics curiously. The trail then bears off to the right, climbs a hill, and rejoins the road about 6 miles from the start. Walk or ski at roadside for about ¼ mile to a pair of chalet-type houses on the left. Here Cobble Hill Trail begins anew, passing between these houses and following a logging road uphill through the pines for a short distance before rejoining the Viking's network of groomed trails. Turn right, and turn right again at the next intersection. This puts you back on the trail which you followed outward bound, and which will take you to the touring center in about 1 mile.

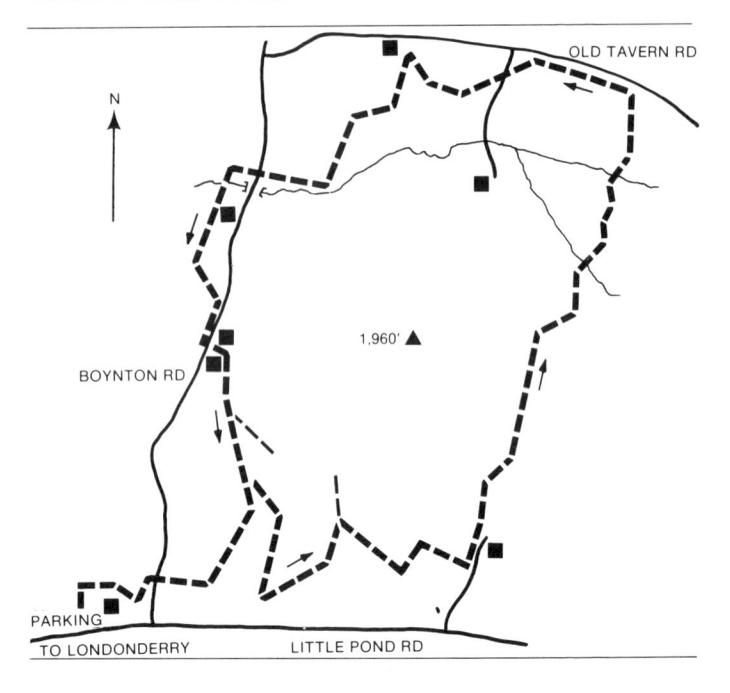

8 Utley Brook Trail

Around the loop: 12 miles

Difficulty: considerable

Map: XC Peru

Make no mistake, this is a wilderness trail over terrain that is often rough, but it was cut and blazed especially for cross-country skiers. You'll meet no snowmobiles except at the near and far ends of the loop, and between times you'll pass through some perfectly magnificent country. Midway, if you decide the trail is too difficult, you can bail out on a Forest Service road that will take you back to civilization in an hour or two, even in the dark.

Drive to Landgrove on an unnumbered road from VT 11 west of Londonderry. (You can also get there from Weston or Peru.) Landgrove is just about the smallest township in Vermont. It was settled by William Utley in 1769 under the impression that he was in Peru; when he realized his mistake, he petitioned the legislature for a township of his own, which was duly granted. Today, Landgrove proper (there is also a North Landgrove, which oddly enough is located to the south of it) consists of a few houses and the Village Inn. Drive to the inn, a sprawling red clapboard structure on the right, and sign the register at the office. A rough trail map published by the Peru Outdoor Recreation Club (donation $1) is available here, as is advice on the condition of the trail. If you

8   Utley Brook Trail

are the cautious type, you will want to supplement the PORC map with a topographical sheet, USGS Wallingford, which will also prove useful for skiing the west end of the Mount Tabor Road (see Tour 9).

The ski trail begins directly behind the inn. Enter the woods at a blue diamond near a child's exercise cage, then turn to the right. The trail soon swings around to the left and climbs a hill, fetching a circuit to a plowed but often skiable road. This takes you down to the Weston

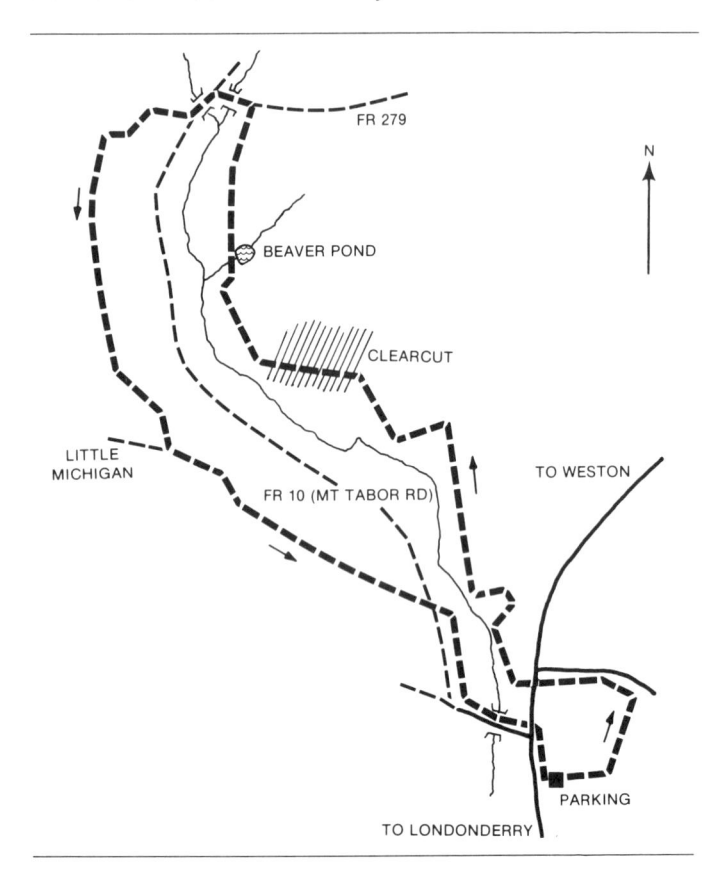

Utley Brook Trail

Road, which is more heavily traveled. Cross it (caution!) and ski through a field on the other side. The trail bears off to the right before settling down to the compass heading it will follow for most of the outbound journey: northwest. After a steep downhill, it reaches a trail junction about 1 mile from the start. The left fork takes you out to the plowed road; the Utley Brook Trail is straight ahead. It's almost level for a considerable stretch, then joins Utley Brook (like many Vermont brooks, a fair-sized river) and jogs uphill to the right. Until now the forest has been mostly evergreen, but this knoll is covered with hardwoods. Descend it on the other side and cross a brook. Again the trail is level for a time, until it crosses a second brook, jogs to the south, and enters a vast clearcut area about 4 miles from the start. Pay attention here: the route was poorly marked when we passed through. If you have no track to follow, keep to the left (south side) along an old logging road, leaving the clearcut at last on a westerly course.

Soon the trail joins the river again, then swings off to the right along a tributary brook, which it follows to a massive beaver dam. Cross on the dam. The trail slabs the side of a hill until it picks up a logging road, which it follows to Forest Road 279, about 6 miles from the start. This road is snowmobiled, crosses Utley Brook on a highway bridge, and is even equipped with a small picnic area. Bear left across the bridge, joining Forest Road 10 in a few hundred feet. This is the Mount Tabor Road (also known as the Danby Road), which will take you back to Landgrove if you find yourself running short of time or energy. Otherwise follow it southeast just long enough to cross the bridge over Lodge Brook, then immediately turn right and enter the woods (The blue diamond marking the trailhead may not be visible from the

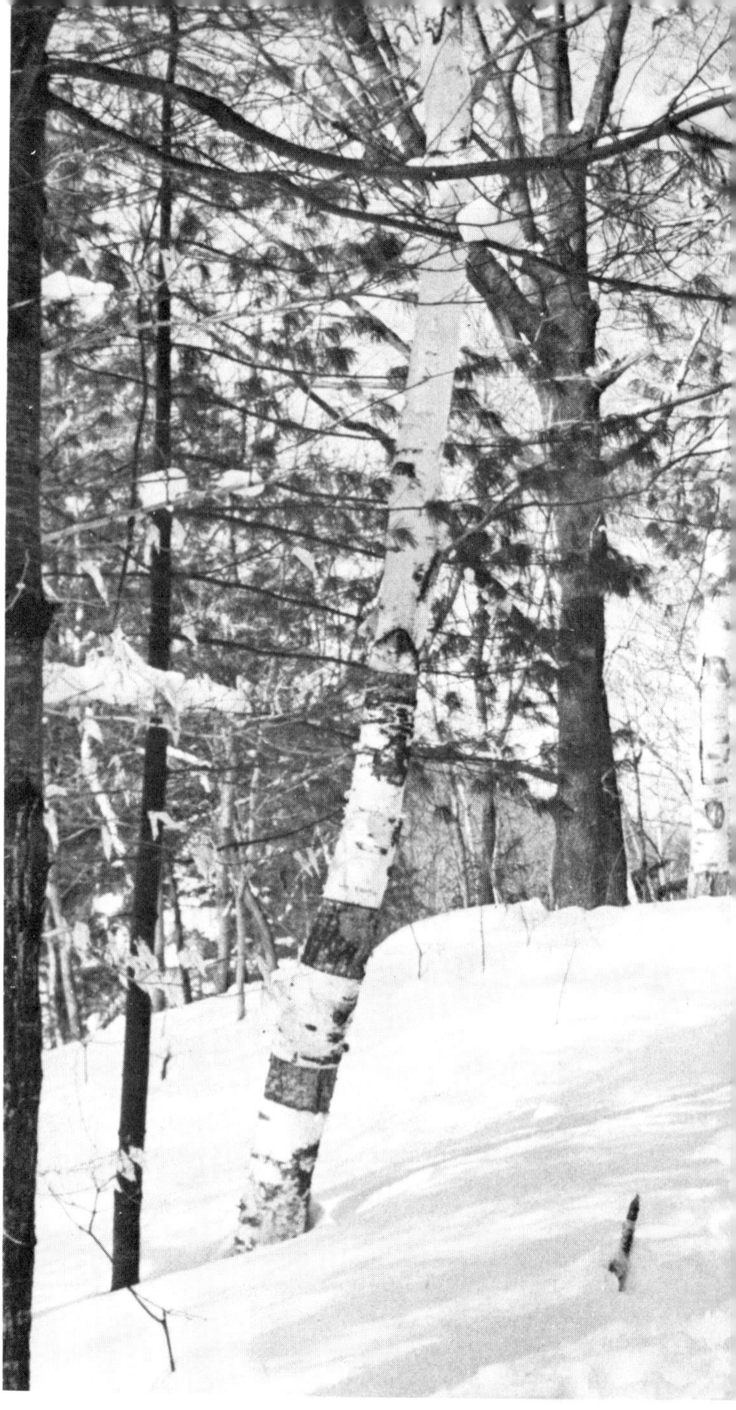

Utley Brook Trail uses old logging roads from time to time

Utley Brook Trail

road.) You now set off on a detour to the west on a logging road, which eventually turns south, then west again. Finally the trail leaves that road for another at the top of a knoll, heading due south.

This leg takes you down to a brook, which you follow for a time, then cross on a footbridge. A long and sporty downhill run brings you to another brook and another bridge, whereupon the trail bears hard right and climbs a hill. Through the hardwoods you can see Holt Mountain to your left (northeast) and Pete Parent Peak behind you (northwest). Then it's back into the evergreens and the junction with Little Michigan Trail on the right, 9 miles from the start. Take heart: the difficult skiing is mostly behind you. The trail slabs the side of a ridge, before dropping downhill through the hardwoods, where you can zig and zag at your pleasure between the wide-spaced trees. Then it's a long slog through the evergreens to Forest Road 10. Turn to the right, then almost immediately enter the woods on the left side of the road. It's a short ski across marshy ground and through a grove of young red pines, with Utley Brook on your left and the road on your right, until you come out on the plowed road just above a bridge, 12 miles from the start. However, you still have a short walk ahead of you, about ¼ mile down Forest Road 10 to the Weston Road, then turn right for another ¼ mile to the Village Inn. Don't forget to sign in at the office.

The record for this trek is 2 hours and 15 minutes, but don't expect to do it in less than twice that time. To be on the safe side, leave the Village Inn by 9 a.m., and if you reach the road intersection much later than noon, ski home by way of Forest Road 10. That could save you (and the members of the Peru Outdoor Recreation Club) considerable anguish.

9 Mount Tabor Road

To bridge and
return: 5 miles

Difficulty:
slight

Map: USGS
Wallingford

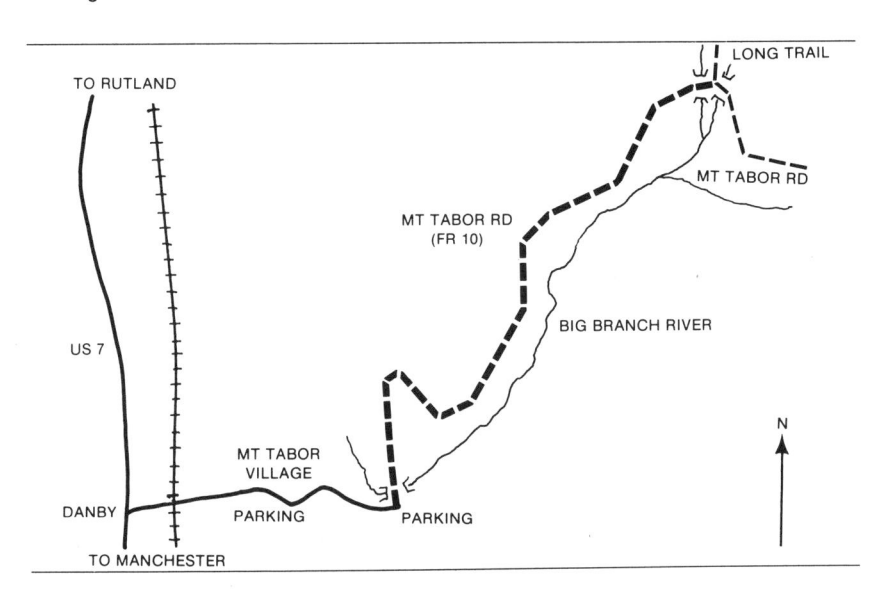

Taken from the west, the Mount Tabor Road leads to a vast ski-touring area. You can strike out on the Long Trail, north or south, or you can follow the road for mile upon mile to its height-of-land at Devil's Den. You can even ski right through to Landgrove (see Tour 8), though how you would return is another matter. Does it sound too perfect to be true? Well, there are some drawbacks: you must share the road with snowmobiles and some-

9 Mount Tabor Road

times with logging trucks, and the parking leaves something to be desired.

Mount Tabor in this case is a village—the mountain for which it was named is many inaccessible miles to the south. To reach the village, follow US 7 to Danby, between Manchester and Rutland. Danby is west of the highway; Mount Tabor lies to the east, across the railroad tracks and past a U.S. Forest Service storage depot. The village is a pretty cluster of houses. You might stop at one of them to inquire about parking and current logging activity. With luck, you'll find a parking spot at the end of the plowed road, just before the bridge over the Big Branch River, where the road makes a sharp left turn and heads due north. Failing that, you'll have to leave your car at roadside in Mount Tabor or attack the snowbank with a shovel, then walk or ski to the end of the plowed section. However you get there, the road

Snowy day on the Mount Tabor Road–Long Trail intersection

9 Mount Tabor Road

climbs to the north at a hearty but skiable pitch, white and yellow birches bordering the right-of-way and allowing glimpses of the Otter Creek Valley to the west. About ½ mile from the start, the road makes a hairpin turn and heads southeast for a time, then bears northeast along the steep side of Green Mountain.

Just as you're thinking it's time to change waxes, the road relents. There's a level stretch, then another climb, and again a level stretch, as if you were ascending a huge flight of stairs. Finally, about 1½ miles from the start, the road swings around to the right and a guardrail invites you to approach the edge and look down into the glen of the Big Branch, whose waters can be heard far below. Across the glen are cliffs no steeper than those upon which the Forest Service built this road. The route is now uphill again, to an overlook and picnic ground about 2 miles from the start. The road then climbs to a high spot where a house is visible through the trees on the right; then it's downhill very briefly to the bridge over Little Black Branch, which is followed almost immediately by the bridge over Big Black Branch.

Between these spans, on the left, is a sign for the northbound section of the Long Trail. An intermediate party can ski along that rough but nearly level footpath for 2 miles to Lula Tye Shelter and Little Rock Pond. Returning from this destination involves a round trip of 9 miles. Alternately, it is possible to ski down the Homer Stone Brook Trail 2 miles to a point near South Wallingford, for total of 6½ miles of skiing. An automobile shuttle is required, and the first part of the Homer Stone Brook Trail is a tricky downhill run. (See the *Guide Book of the Long Trail,* published by the Green Mountain Club, for a sketch map and trail descriptions.)

9   Mount Tabor Road

Southbound, the Long Trail coincides with the Mount Tabor Road for a short distance, then leaves it on the right. Rather than follow the hiking path, you can continue along the road for about 1 mile to a woods road on the right, the former route of the Long Trail and the one that is shown on the USGS quadrangle. In just under ½ mile, this road leads to the Big Branch suspension bridge on the Long Trail, which will take you west (downstream) to Big Branch Shelter in about 200 yards. The round trip is about 8 miles. (Again, see the *Guide Book of the Long Trail* for details.) If you prefer to stay on the Forest Service road, the road is generally uphill and eastward to Devil's Den, about 8 miles from the start and involving a vertical climb of about 1,400 feet. Only a very strong party, with a long day and good weather, should attempt this variant.

10 Northam Shelter

To shelter and return: 7 miles

Difficulty: moderate

Map: USGS Killington Pk.

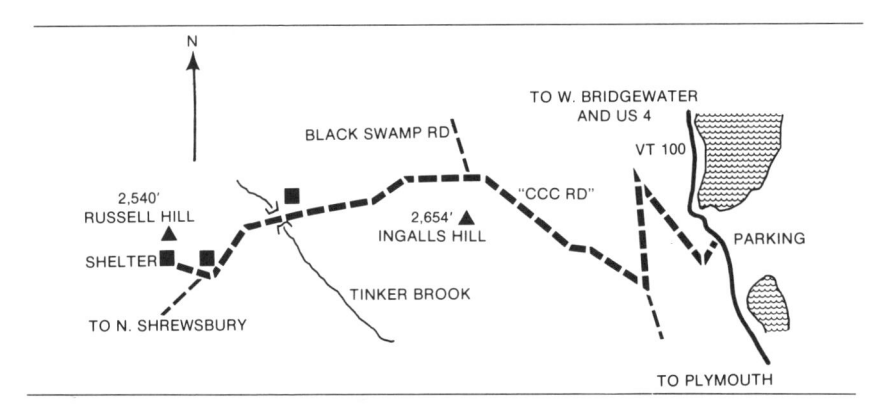

During the Great Depression, the Civilian Conservation Corps kept young men out of trouble and in the process changed the face of the American wilderness. One of their projects may be seen in Calvin Coolidge State Forest near Plymouth, in the form of a picnic area and a mountain road. The latter is now called the "Old CCC Road"—so far have we come in forty years. It's shown as a recreational highway on the Vermont state map. Approach it from VT 100, 1¾ miles north of Round Top ski area or 3¼ miles south of its junction with US 4. The CCC Road is on the west side of the highway at a double curve, just below the rocky headland that encloses Woodward Reservoir. Nothing distinguishes the road except a sign indicating that the legal weight limit is 24,000 pounds. Usually there is ample room to park on VT 100 without interfering with the travel lane, either immediately north or immediately south of the trailhead.

It's a steep climb for the first 2 miles, so put on your best wax and ski uphill to the left. Almost immediately the road jogs back to the right (northwest) and climbs the mountainside in brisk fashion, crossing a brook and then swinging back to the south again. About 1 mile from the start there's another hairpin turn, this one with a logging road continuing straight ahead. You have gained about 600 vertical feet with these switchbacks, so more than half your labor has already been accomplished. Meanwhile the views to the east have been opening up. Throughout, the CCC Road has been marked with the orange triangles and streamers that indicate a snowmobile route, and you will probably find the snow compacted the full width of the road.

Near the height-of-land, about 2 miles from the start, Black Swamp Road comes in from the right, and henceforth you will find many trails coming in from right and left, all of them popular with snowmobilers. The CCC Road heads almost due west at this point, dropping downhill and providing a sudden view of Killington Peak to the northwest; the cleared areas below the summit are downhill ski trails. Straight ahead you can see Russell Hill, which is your destination. In the meantime, however, you must drop down about 200 vertical feet to Tinker Brook, passing a fine stone house on the right. Climbing uphill again through a spruce forest—the first evergreens on this tour—you'll soon spot a large brown structure off in the woods, 3½ miles from the start. This is a picnic pavilion built by the CCC. You can use it for that purpose, or—if the snowmobiles are too numerous for your

Backcountry touring can take you through trackless new snow ▶

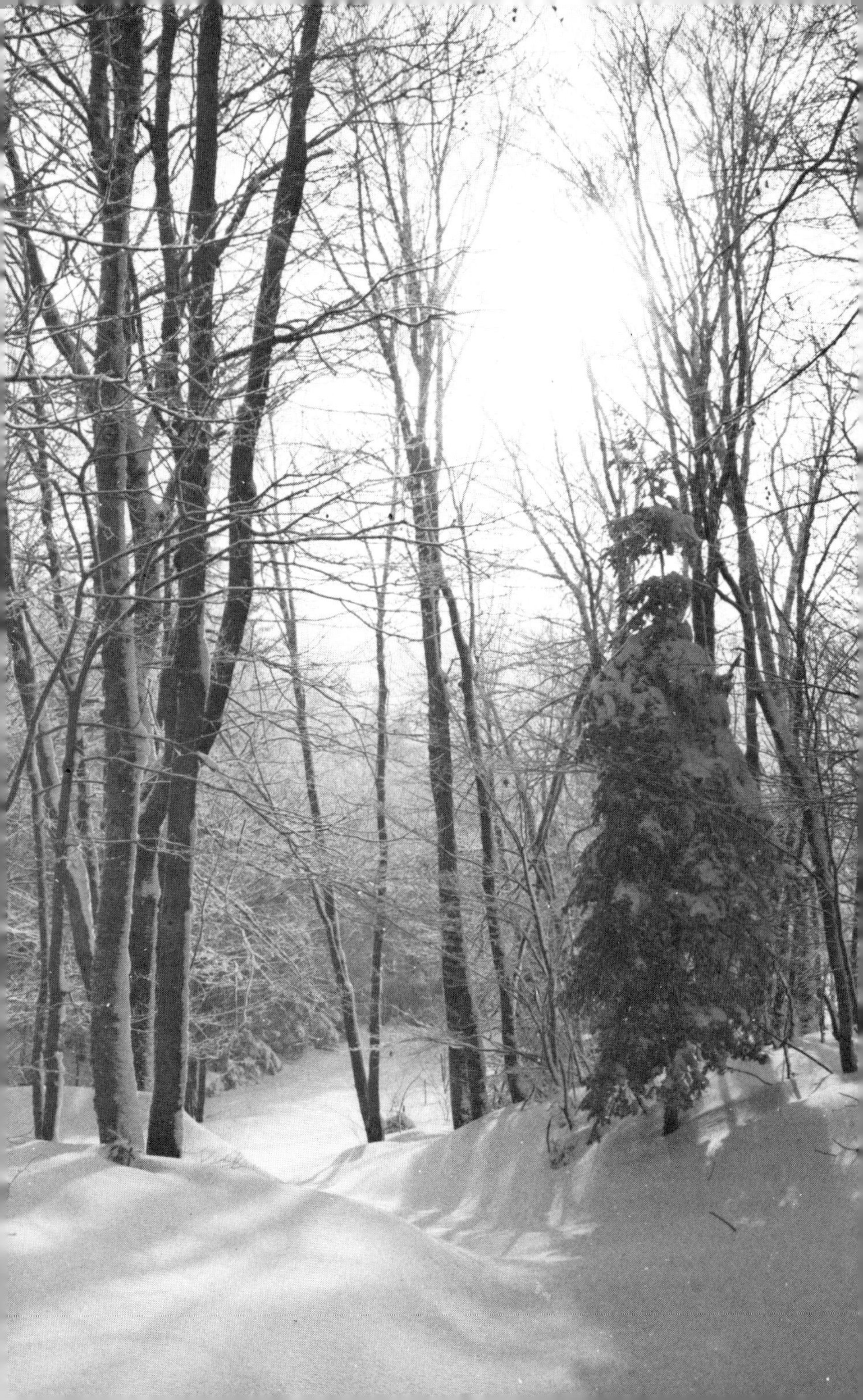

10 Northam Shelter

taste—you can bushwhack up the hill behind the picnic area (northwest). This is Russell Hill, and just below its summit is Northam Shelter, a most unusual lean-to designed to accommodate six campers. One or two more can bunk in the loft, reached by a ladder and completely protected from the weather. If you've ever been tempted to try winter camping, Northam Shelter would provide a snug beginning. It also provides an opportunity to study the industrious porcupine at work, stripping the bark from nearby trees—not to mention fine views to the southeast. One of those rounded summits is 3,278-foot Saltash Mountain.

Northam is the old name for North Shrewsbury, a community which has since gravitated several miles to the southwest. Early in the nineteenth century, the hill farmers used to gather here for worship, there being no proper church available to them. We searched diligently for the site but could not find it. Perhaps you'll do better, so we pass along the description from the Depression-era guidebook to Vermont: "Meeting-House Rock, left from picnic area over a newly cut footpath, is a large flat-topped boulder where, in 1818, Elder Abiatha Knapp conducted divine service, weather permitting. . . . The rough stone benches reserved for the choir and the elders have lately been restored."

Returning to VT 100, remember that you must climb about 200 vertical feet to the height-of-land. As you ski down from the height-of-land, you'll find that some sections are steep enough, especially toward the bottom, that you may prefer to bear off into the soft snow in the woods. Generally the hardwoods are open enough to permit this kind of roaming.

11 Mount Tom

To summit and return: 4½ miles

Difficulty: slight

Map: XC Woodstock

Woodstock is a town with the agreeable smell of what New Englanders like to call "old money." This ski tour was made possible by a combination of two nineteenth century fortunes, one accumulated by Frederick Billings of the Northern Pacific Railroad, the other by John D. Rockefeller of Standard Oil. Mr. Billings was first on the ground. He purchased a handsome acreage that included the bluff-sided Mount Tom, overlooking the village green, and he built carriage roads so that his guests could roam the estate with the least possible inconvenience. Now the summit of Mount Tom is a park, and the acres surrounding it have become a tree farm and ski-touring center owned by one of Mr. Rockefeller's grandsons. It adds a bit of spice, somehow, to know that you are skiing on Rockefeller land. And the outlook at the summit is a rare combination of wealthy homes, working farms, distant mountains, and the nearby shops and hostelries of Woodstock.

Begin your quest at the Woodstock Ski Touring Center—otherwise the country club—located on VT 106 about ½ mile south of the Woodstock Inn and the village green. Go around to the rear of this handsome building and you

Mount Tom

Mount Tom offers views of town and country

11   Mount Tom

will find a ski shop, where you can pay your trail fee ($2 at this writing) and obtain a sketch map of the Mount Tom trails. Then drive back to the village green, turn right on US 4, and almost immediately turn left again on VT 12 heading north. This road takes you over the Ottauquechee River, past a Rockefeller home and the Mount Tom ski area (both on the left), and eventually to a historical marker which is worth a pause for reflection. Here, on the right side of the road, in Clinton Gilbert's pasture, the first uphill ski lift in the United States went into operation in January 1934, powered by a Model T engine. It was a historic moment, dividing the sport of skiing into two very different sports, "downhill" and "cross-country." What a confusion of equipment, clothing, and skills has resulted from that moment!

Just beyond the marker (and 4 miles from the touring center) there is an unpaved road on the left, with a sign pointing to West Woodstock. Follow this road uphill for about ¾ mile to a parking lot on the left. Walk or ski along the road for a few hundred yards to the beginning of the carriage road. It is rather steep to begin with, but soon settles into a more gentle pitch, leading you through a grove of pines about sixty years old, then through hardwoods with views to the north. After crossing a stone bridge, the carriage road levels off and enters pine woods again. This forest is actively managed by the Rockefeller interests, providing firewood for the inn and timber for new construction. Test borings have shown some of the hemlocks to be four hundred years old.

About ½ mile from the start, the road forks. Turn right, and turn right again at the next intersection. This takes you gently downhill past a pond called The Pogue (*a loop trail goes around the pond*) and to a final intersec-

Mount Tom

tion about 1 mile from the start. There is a small green building here and a sign for the summit of Mount Tom. Turn right and climb through a field; you'll soon enter the evergreen woods again, with yellow-spotted hiking trails branching off to the left. This indicates that you have left Rockefeller land and have entered a public park. One of the trails leads to the main summit of Mount Tom, and with good snow conditions can be negotiated by intermediate skiers. For its part, the carriage road drops downhill, crosses a marvelous stone causeway, and climbs again to the south summit, where it makes a loop with splendid views to the east, south, and west. If the snow is not too deep, you'll be able to lean your skis against the hitching posts that held the horses of nineteenth-century gentlefolk.

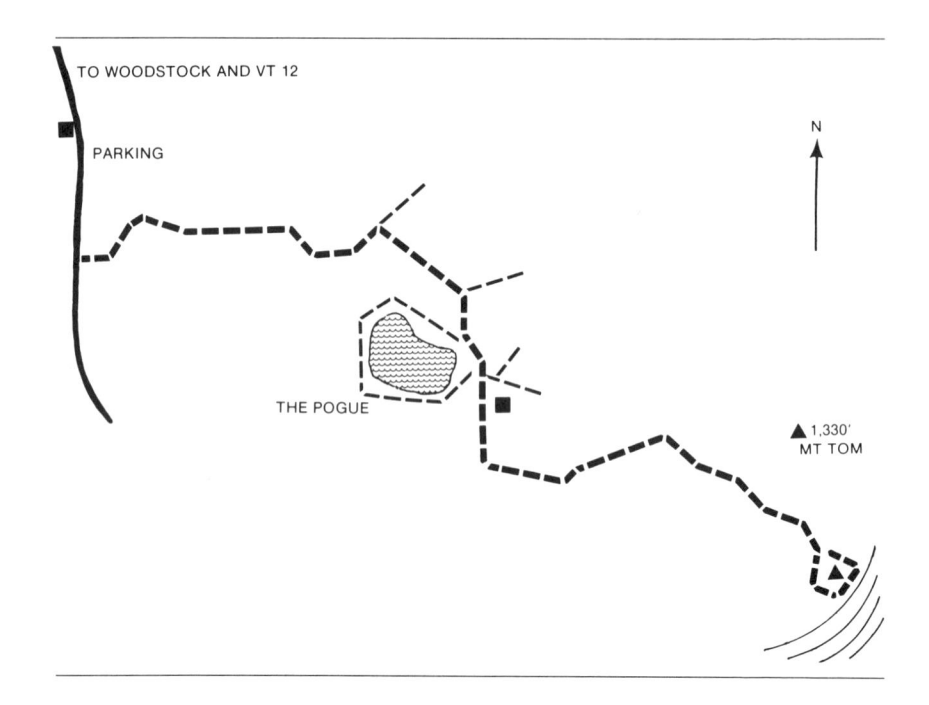

11 Mount Tom

Return the way you came or take one of the variants shown on the sketch map. Any of these trails can be negotiated by a good novice skier, given decent snow conditions.

12 Webster Hill

To vista and return: 4 miles

Difficulty: moderate

Map: USGS Woodstock N.

What can one person do to improve a busy world? Quite a bit, to judge by the ski tracks we found at Amity Pond Natural Area, a few miles north of Woodstock. The area was given to the state by Richard Brett on the condition that machines be "forever barred." Not content with preserving a corner of Vermont from the internal combustion engine, Mr. Brett joined a few other stalwarts to cut the Skyline Trail for cross-country skiers. It is located mostly on private land, but uses Amity Pond Natural Area as a way station, and that is where we suggest you join it. The first 2 miles southbound will take you along a ridge commanding some of the most magnificent scenery in this corner of New England.

Take VT 12 north from Woodstock, and in about 1 mile bear right at a Texaco station for South Pomfret. This village is reached in about 2 miles; turn right for the second time at a Mobil station and general store. In 5 miles look for the Moore farm, with a large white house and a sign for farm produce. Turn *left* here at a sign for Sharon and East Barnard. In about ⅓ mile turn left again onto a dirt road known locally as the Mail Route. It will take you in just over 2 miles to Amity Pond Natural Area, located

12   Webster Hill

at the crown of a hill and identified by some orange no-snowmobile signs on the left. Park as best you can, at the widest spot available. (The nearest turnaround is ½ mile down the road.)

Mr. Brett built a lean-to shelter where brochures and a register were available, but by the time we came this way the shelter had been burned by careless campers. Happily they paid for the damage, so the shelter—and trail maps—may once again be available. In any event, you will be as well served by the topographical sheet and our sketch map. The Skyline Trail is marked by large wooden diamonds painted blue and orange. Southbound

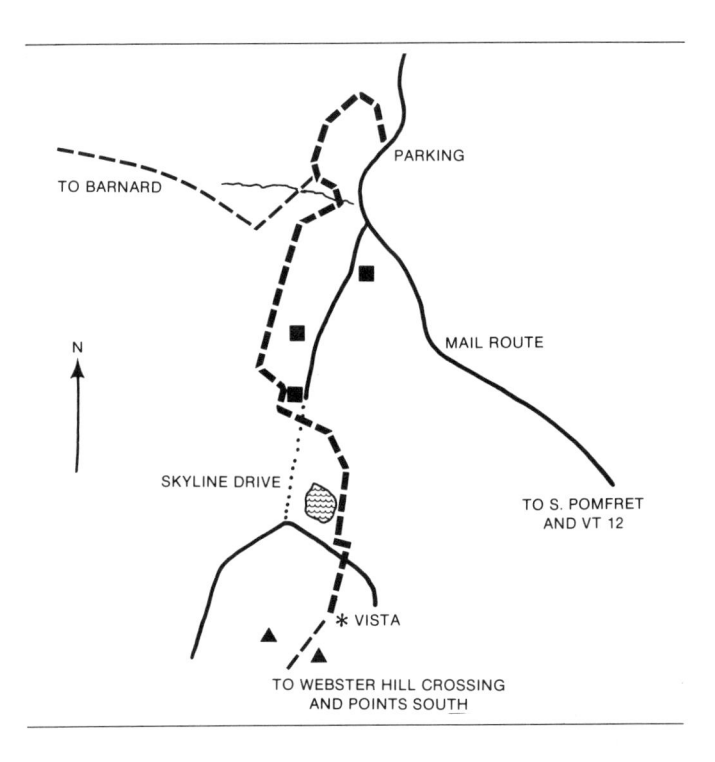

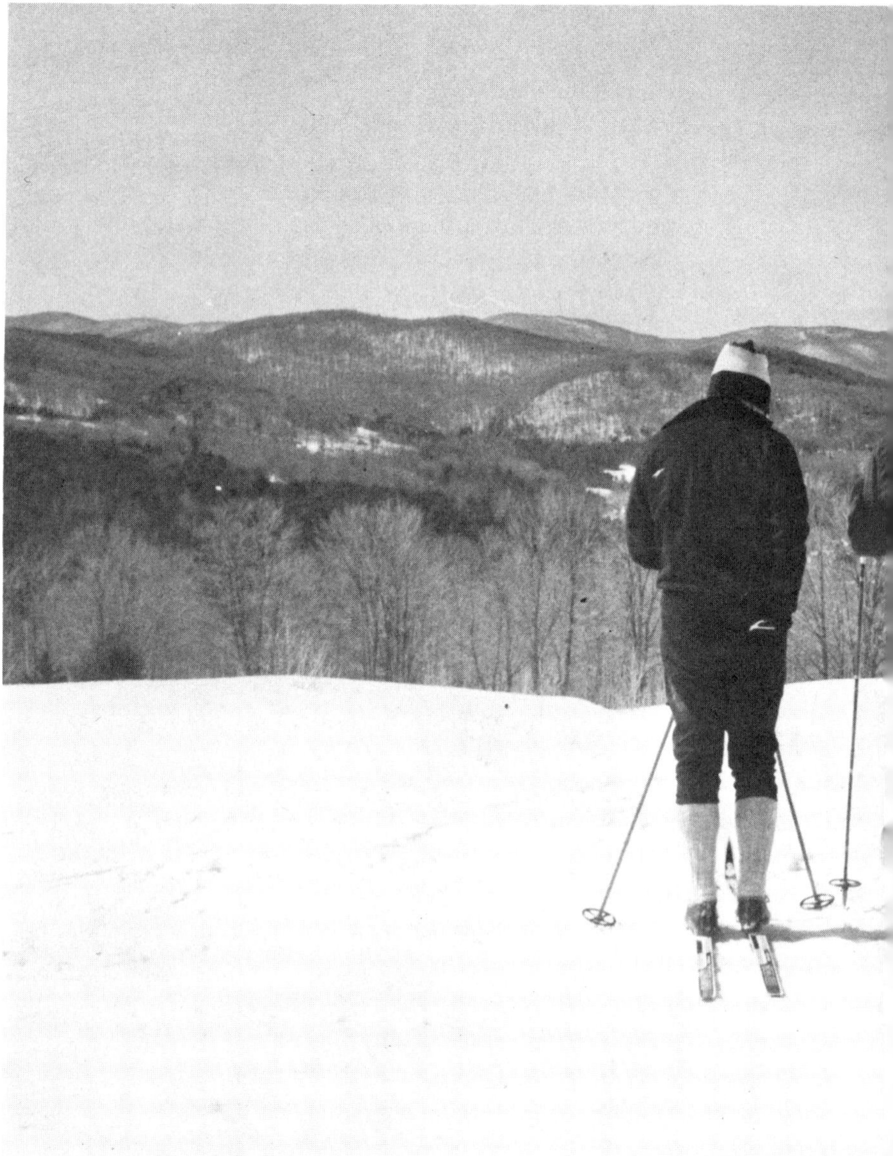

12   Webster Hill

The Green Mountains from Amity Pond Natural Area

12 Webster Hill

for Webster Hill, you'll want the blue sector on top. The beginning of the trail is a loop around to the north, to avoid a gully; it takes you out to an open hill with wide views of the mountains to the west. Turn left (south) and you should see a house with a metal roof that is your first target. Ski downhill, keeping to the left, and you'll come to a clump of white birches with a trail sign in front of them. Take the left fork, where the signboard is painted blue and marked for Woodstock. (At this writing, the Skyline Trail goes about half the distance.) It leads you down into a gully and up again toward that metal-roofed house. You'll pass well to the right of it, however. The marked route leads through a post-and-rail fence, with the rails removed for your convenience, then under a power line and through the fence on the other side. There's a brief downhill, then you're traveling almost due south along a farm road fringed by trees.

Coming out into the open, you may find that ridgelines have the disadvantage of being swept by the wind. There's a log house ahead; pass fairly close to it on the right, then bear left uphill toward a pretty white house with a red roof. Our trail map showed us as crossing the plowed Skyline Drive at this point, but the marked route kept us west of the road so that we passed embarrassingly close to the house—we can only assume the owners are very fond of skiers. We continued south for a few hundred yards, then crossed the Skyline Drive at a point where it was no longer plowed, about 1¼ miles from the start. From here the trail meanders east and south through a pasture now filling with young pines. Then there's a sporty downhill run to a pond, which you cross on the dam at the east end. The trail now emerges on a plowed dirt road. Turn left and ski along the embankment for a few hundred feet, then cross over and climb steeply uphill on what appears to be a snowmobile race-

12 Webster Hill

way. At the height-of-land you'll see a view to the east. Turn left here and go out on the open area for a panorama that may include the snow-capped heights of Mount Lafayette to the northeast, nearly sixty miles away. (On an exceptionally clear day, you can also see Mount Washington beyond.) Besides the White Mountains, peaks visible along the Skyline Trail include the downhill ski areas on Ascutney to the southeast and Killington and Pico to the southwest.

From our recommended stopping place, the trail drops down to Webster Hill Crossing, then makes a loop about 4 miles around, over country that is sometimes arduous and along routes that are sometimes hard to follow. (There is one spectacular hill to climb; from its bald summit there is one of the few 360° views to be found in the Green Mountain State.) We commend this trail only to strong skiers with a clear track to follow and a full day at their disposal. The total distance is only 8 miles, but there's considerable activity along the way.

Returning from the lookout, pay close attention to the trail. The markers are now orange on top. From the plowed road, you enter the woods at a no-trespassing sign (!); once on the ridge to the west of Skyline Drive, remember that your course is generally north-northeast toward the large open hill where you began. These precautions are necessary because both skiers and snowmobiles have crisscrossed the route, and because the wind can erase your own tracks within an hour. If in doubt, go out to the Skyline Drive and follow it to the Mail Route, then turn left for your automobile.

13 Gifford Woods

Distance: 1–2 miles

Difficulty: slight

Map: none needed

Oddly enough, no one really knows what the New England forest looked like before the seventeenth century, when the Europeans began to cut it down. We can only guess. Early travelers wrote of driving their wagons between the trees, mile after mile—a notion almost impossible to grasp for those of us who have bushwhacked through today's backcountry. (There must have been patches of second-growth timber in the primeval forest, too. Lighting strikes could set the woods ablaze, and the Indians used controlled burning as a tool to clear farmland and fertilize it at the same time.) From such testimony, and from what we can see in the oldest woodlots available to us, we can guess that such trees were often one hundred feet apart, and that they reached seventy-five feet into the air before branching; at the top, the foliage interlocked to throw the forest floor into near-darkness. When a tree fell because of disease or old age, young saplings raced to fill the gap. The victor earned a place in the sun; the others died. Thus the dominant growth was nothing like the gnarled "pasture pine" or "boundary oak" that we regard as ancient, but trees that were as slender as they were straight. Or so we assume—not every forester agrees with this picture.

13   Gifford Woods

A hint of the primeval forest can be found in Gifford Woods, a Vermont state park which also happens to be on the route of a commercial ski-touring center. Thus there's free access, thanks to state park policy, and a groomed track, thanks to the touring center. To reach the main body of the park, follow VT 100 north for about ½ mile after it parts company with US 4, not far from the access road to Killington ski area. Keep an eye peeled for the state highway: it looks like a country lane, dropping downhill at Bill's Country Store. On the right (east) side of the road, across from the park maintenance shop, you'll find a plowed space for five or six cars. (Alternately, you can reach Gifford Woods from the Mountain Meadows Ski Touring Center. It's located on Thundering Brook Road, paralleling VT 100 to the east, and the trail fee at this writing is $2.50.)

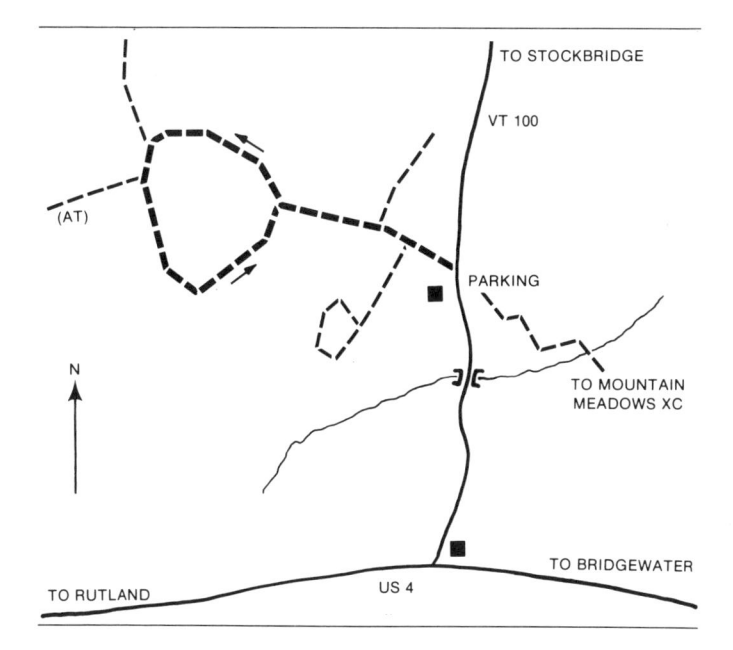

13   Gifford Woods

Cross the pavement and enter the woods at a sign for the Appalachian Trail, which is marked with blue paint blazes within the park. It coincides with the access road, used in summertime by campers and picnickers. Ski straight ahead and uphill on this road, leaving a side-

Entering Gifford Woods on the Appalachian Trail

13   Gifford Woods

road on the left and a woods trail on the right. Both these routes are groomed for skiing: the first leads to a camping area near the maintenance shop, the second to a motel about ½ mile distant. Both are rated novice, but the "Grey Bonnet Loop" to the right is up and down through young hardwoods, and therefore a bit more difficult to ski.

The main park loop continues uphill, with the return leg coming in from the left. A gigantic boulder and a fine hemlock grove are also on the left, not to mention picnic tables and lean-to shelters. At the top of the hill, another ski trail bears off to the right, also leading to the Grey Bonnet Motel, but rated intermediate. Almost immediately thereafter, a blue arrow and blue paint blazes show where the Appalachian Trail bears off to the south and its beginning at Springer Mountain in Georgia, about 1,750 miles away. Through much of Vermont, the AT coincides with the Long Trail, but here in Gifford Woods they have diverged, with the Long Trail continuing north along the spine of the Green Mountains while the AT heads east for the White Mountains of New Hampshire.

By all means ski into the hemlock grove on the inside of this circle. The trees are handsome, averaging two feet in diameter. Somewhere in Gifford Woods, or so we were told, there is the great-grandfather of all hemlocks, four feet in diameter. Alas, we couldn't find him, but his arrow-straight descendants were impressive enough.

14 Reservoir Loop

Around the
loop: 8 miles

Difficulty:
moderate

Map: XC
Mountain Top

If so many of our tours seem to lead up a mountain and down again, it's because Vermont has a definite tendency toward the vertical. Green Mountain valleys are usually wide enough for a river, a road, and a farm. If you want to go a-touring, you must cross the high ground between one valley and the next. Here's a welcome change: a circuit 8 miles around, with all but the last 2 miles rolling pleasantly over a valley floor. In the midst of all is the Chittenden Reservoir, a power source for the Central Vermont Public Service Company. The trail is marked (but not groomed or patrolled) by the Mountain Top Ski Touring Center in Chittenden, which at this writing charges a $2.50 trail fee, map included. To reach the touring center, drive to Chittenden on an unnumbered road from US 7, north of Rutland, or from US 4 to the east. Five roads come together in the village. Take the central fork to the Mountain Top Inn. The inn was closed when we were there, but the touring center was in fine shape, dispensing coffee, advice, and other necessaries from a stove-heated outbuilding on the left.

After signing out, walk or ski back toward the inn, then head north on a plowed road for about 200 yards past some rental cottages. The plowed section soon ends,

Reservoir Loop

with the road continuing as a ski and snowmobile trail downhill to a bridge over Hewitt Brook. It then climbs at an easy grade to a field, a ruined house, and a junction. Here, about 1½ miles from the start, the New Boston Trail continues northward and the Round Robin ski trail branches off to the right (east). Follow the latter into an old road now growing to scrub. It is marked both with blue diamonds as a ski trail and with yellow (sometimes orange) diamonds as a snowmobile route. Soon it leads between two ruined farm buildings. From the open stretches there are views of Mount Carmel, like a sugarloaf to the north, and Pico Peak to the south. The trail now leads downhill, makes a dogleg to the left, and enters another overgrown field and orchard, with splendid views through an arc of 270°. At the end of this field,

A deer and rabbit left the only tracks this morning

Reservoir Loop

about 2½ miles from the start, the trail swings south to enter the evergreen forest. It soon crosses a bridge, then another and more elaborate span, and settles down on a long slog southward. The forest changes from evergreen to hardwood and back again, with occasional glimpses of the reservoir on your right. All brook crossings are nicely bridged, and altogether we remember this as one of the best-engineered ski trails we have ever followed. It's worth noting that the touring center and a local snowmobile club cooperated in doing the work.

Finally, about 5 miles from the start, there is a trail junction, with the left fork heading off toward Mountain Mead-

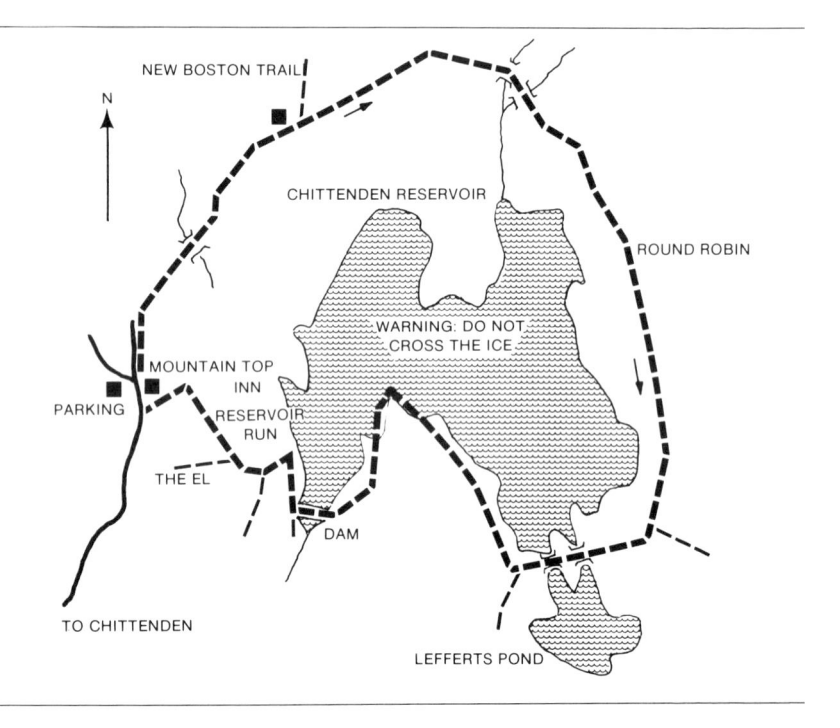

14   Reservoir Loop

ows Ski Touring Center, 12 long miles away. For your part, keep right and follow a woods road to the west between Chittenden Reservoir and Lefferts Pond. Two brooks connect these bodies of water. After the second bridge there are fine views of the multi-peaked Blue Ridge Mountain to the south, while northward you can see Mount Carmel with a large clearcut area on its flank. Shortly thereafter, the snowmobile route bears off to the left and Round Robin turns sharp right (north) along the shore of the reservoir. This section is a woodland trail, very rough and steep at times, and it can be hard to follow without a track. If you lose the trail, bushwhack down to the shore and follow it around, but do not venture very far onto the ice. The reservoir is sometimes drawn down for hydroelectric generation, leaving a gap of several feet between the ice and the water. (Do not, under any circumstances, attempt a shortcut across the reservoir.)

The trail ends temporarily at a cove. Following the shore, ski around the northernmost spur of land and reenter the woods at a cove on the opposite side. This leg is also mean, but it is considerably shorter, soon joining an old quarry road which leads you down to Chittenden Dam, about 7 miles from the start. Cross the dam on the catwalk, then head north again on a shore road between the reservoir and a row of cottages. This road swings southward and forks at a gravel pit. Round Robin heads off to the right (west) and ends at a trail junction with The El and Reservoir Run, both leading back to the touring center. Reservoir Run is slightly shorter, and by this time you're probably ready to accept that concession. It will take you through a pretty woodlot, generally uphill, to a field behind the barrack-like Mountain Top Inn. Ski to the left of the inn, and follow the road back to the touring center.

15 Chittenden Brook

Around the loop: 6½ miles

Difficulty: moderate

Map: XC Chittenden Bk.

Thomas Chittenden was the "unlearned, uneloquent, informal giant of a man" who governed Vermont during the years of its independence, 1778–1791, and for five years thereafter. His son Martin later filled the same office and with the same free spirit: during the War of 1812, Vermont pursued its own foreign policy with such dismaying results that the U.S. Congress debated whether it should bring the second Governor Chittenden to trial. Vermonters revered them, father and son. Thus the county, town, reservoir, brook, and U.S. Forest Service recreation area that bear the Chittenden name.

The Forest Service has blazed a ski-touring trail to the Chittenden Brook campground, utilizing old logging roads for the most part. Combined with the campground access road, Forest Road 45, this trail makes a fine loop through the hardwood forest, with occasional views to the north and east. The trailhead is on the south side of VT 73, about 5½ miles west of its junction with VT 100 near Rochester. (Eastbound, it's about the same distance from Goshen Four Corners.) Look for a plowed parking space, a Forest Service sign, and West Hill Road coming in from the north. Sign in at the register box and take a copy of the map-brochure prepared by the Rochester

15 Chittenden Brook

Ranger District, then ski due south on the campground road. In less than 1 mile, shortly after crossing the second of two bridges, you'll see a trail marker on your right. At this point the campground road leads uphill rather steeply, and a logging road veers off to the left.

Well marked by the traditional blue diamonds, the ski trail follows the east bank of Chittenden Brook, climbing

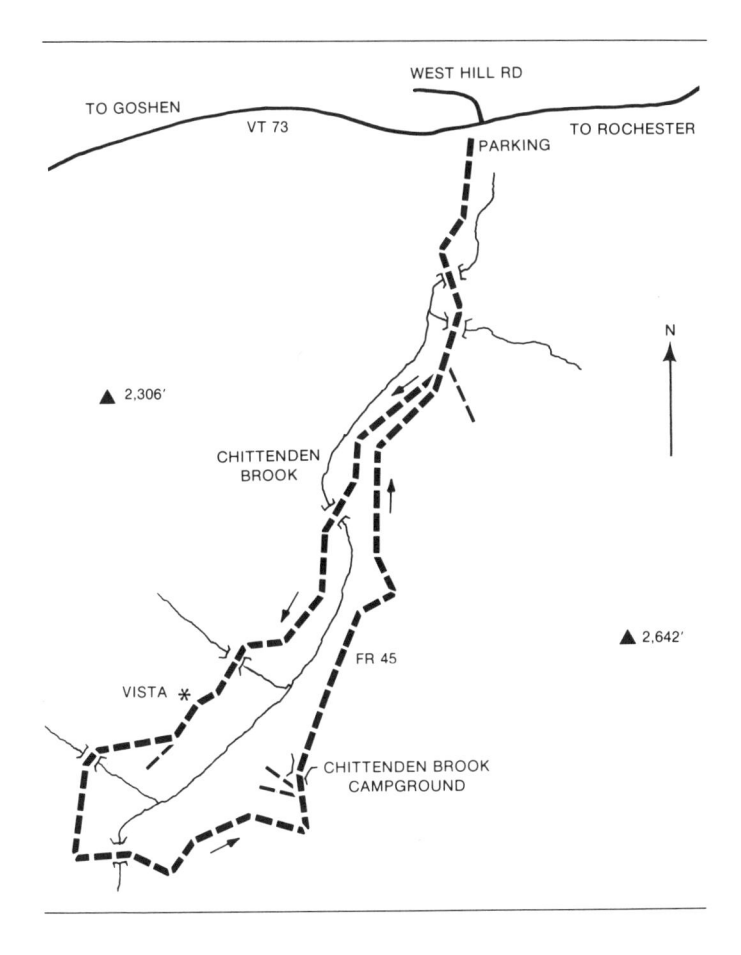

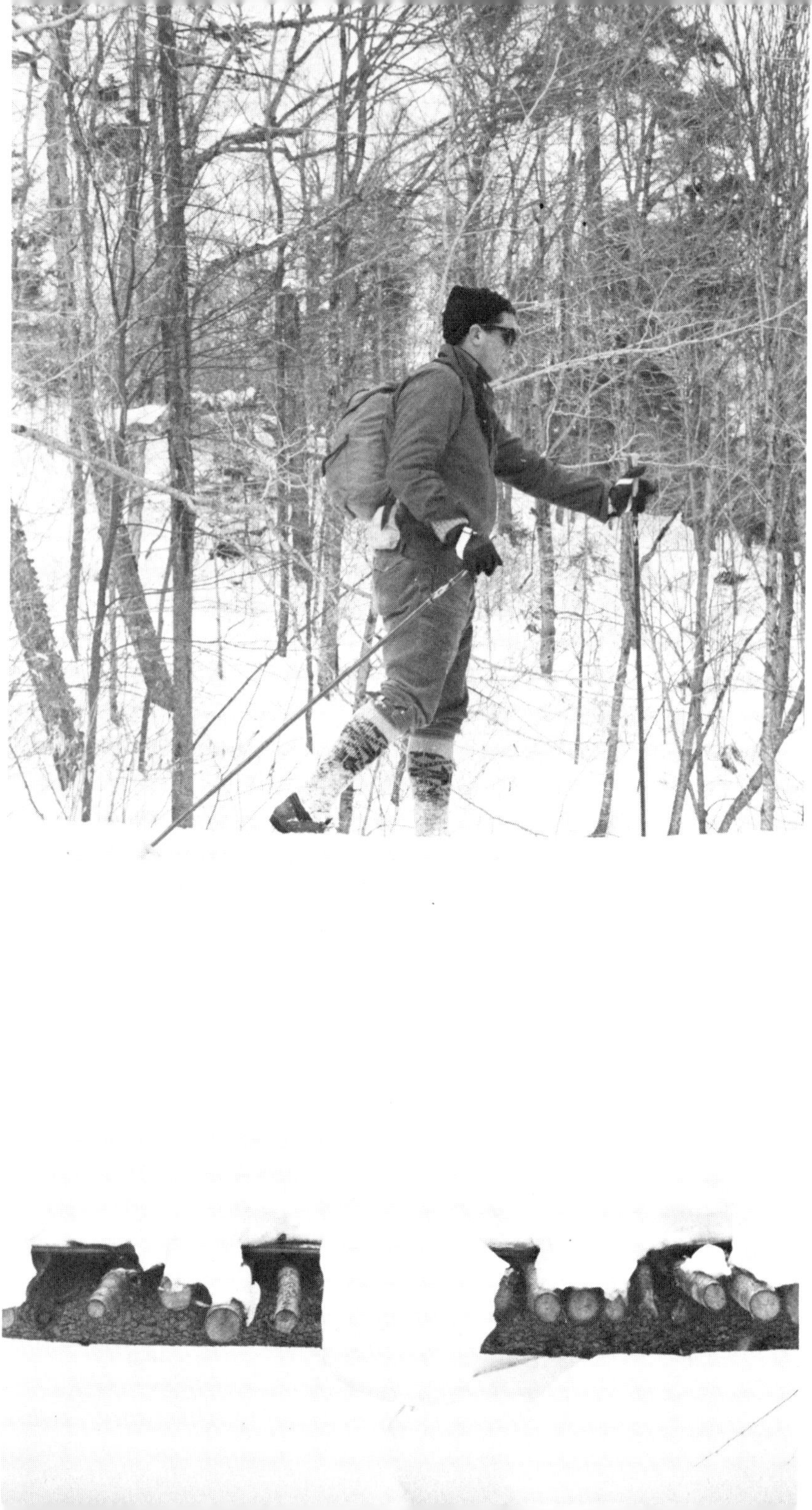

Chittenden Brook

easily. Then, after a steeper section, it crosses to the west bank on a footbridge. There are fine yellow birches all along the route, and as you climb higher you'll see summits to the southeast: Corporation Mountain, Round Mountain, and associated hillocks. The trail then jogs up a tributary brook, swings left to cross it, and levels off before entering an old clearcut or blowdown area, about 2½ miles from the start. For less ambitious skiers, this vista could well serve as a goal, for the trail ahead is much longer than it appears on the map.

After leaving the open area, the trail divides at a sign reading "Alternate Loop." Take the right fork for easier going. The trail climbs for a short distance, then quits the woods road it has been following until now. Turn left, ski sharply downhill to a footbridge, and climb to another and larger open area, now starting to grow to scrub. Here the views include Little Pico to the north. Pay close attention to the blue streamers that mark the trail through the scrub—it's not always obvious if you don't have a track to follow. The trail leads up and down along the ridge in a southerly direction, then drops steeply again to cross yet another bridge. (Here, about the midpoint of the trail, the Forest Service maintains a first-aid cache.) Finally you come upon a woods road at right angles to the trail. Turn to the left and ski north for Chittenden Brook campground, about 4 miles from the start. On this final leg of the trail, we encountered many unbridged gullies which slowed us down but otherwise posed no problem. They might be troublesome in springtime, however.

At the campground, a loop road bears off to your left and returns again to the same spot. To ski back to the highway, face straight ahead (north) and cross a bridge on Forest Road 45. The road drops nearly 500 feet in the

◀ Four feet of snow on the bridge over Chittenden Brook

15   Chittenden Brook

next 1½ miles—a gorgeous run with plenty of space to maneuver in, even when the road is at its steepest. It levels off where you left it for the ski trail, then takes you back to your car as you came.

16 Silver Lake

To lake and
return: 4 miles

Difficulty:
moderate

Map: USGS
E. Middlebury

Silver Lake is a popular destination for skiers, who come in from the east (from Blueberry Hill touring center) and from the south (via the Leicester Hollow Trail). Less frequently taken is the steep but graded road that leads up from Lake Dunmore, past the Falls of Lana, and so to the Silver Lake Dam from the northwest. It's a particularly beautiful tour. Reaching the trailhead is a bit complicated, which may explain the scarcity of ski tracks in that direction: pick up VT 53 at its beginning on US 7, about 7 miles south of Middlebury. (The road can also be approached from VT 73 on the south, between Brandon and Goshen.) At the start, VT 53 is identified as the Lake Dunmore Road, soon transforming itself into West Shore Drive. It skirts the northern tip of the lake and then heads due south. About 4 miles from US 7, you'll see Branbury State Park on your right (west side of the road). The trailhead is about ¼ mile beyond the state park, on your left (east side of the road). It's marked by a yellow gate which prevents automobiles from entering in the summertime, and by a small sign describing the Silver Lake Recreation Area. There's no parking at the trailhead. We found a plowed parking area about 200 yards north, on the same side of the road, sufficient for three or four cars.

Overleaf: Sucker Brook or the Falls of Lana—what's in a name?

16 Silver Lake

Silver Lake

Silver Lake

Failing that, you can probably find a parking space at the plowed entrance to the state park, then walk or ski along the road to the trailhead.

The pitch is extremely steep to begin with, though it soon becomes more reasonable; you may prefer to walk the first hundred yards. At the first bend you'll encounter a sign that informs you: "This area is closed to motor vehicles to provide the quiet and solitude so rare in our daily lives." It's a lovely thought, somewhat marred by the likelihood that sooner or later you'll meet a snowmobile in the Silver Lake reserve.

After a double hairpin turn, the road levels off and passes through a power company right-of-way, affording a handsome view of Lake Dunmore. We found a multitude of deer tracks and droppings all through this area,

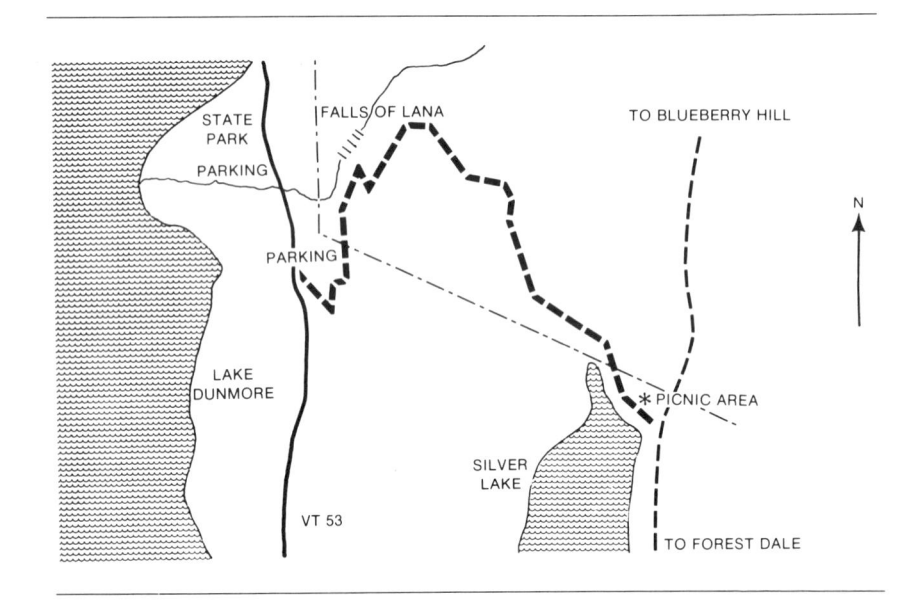

16 Silver Lake

so look for wildlife as you go. After reentering the woods, the road passes close to the gorge of Sucker Brook. If you find that an unromantic name for such a pretty spot, you're in good company: in 1850 General Wool of the U.S. Army visited the cascades and decided to give them a more seemly title than "Sucker Brook Falls." In Mexico he'd been known as General Lana—*lana* being the Spanish for *wool*—so the Falls of Lana they became. Be cautious if you explore them on skis, for the banks are precipitous. The cascades are about ½ mile from the start, and the trail now turns sharply to the right and uphill. Skiing on, you'll negotiate another double hairpin turn, with glimpses of Lake Dunmore to the west and a rocky knob to the north. This peak is known as Rattlesnake Point.

Suddenly you leave the evergreen forest for the hardwoods. Having experienced the change, you'll understand why so many Vermont hills have a hedgehog appearance, with the deciduous trees projecting from the snow like so many quills. The transition is often abrupt, as it is here. Finally the road levels off, drops down to a beaver pond, then climbs again with the power company right-of-way visible through the trees. Do not cross over to the right-of-way until the trail leads you very definitely in that direction. At the crossing, Silver Lake Dam will be in sight ahead. Ski to the left of the dam and along the shore of the lake, through the birches to a picnic area about 2 miles from the start.

Beyond the picnic area you'll find a ski and snowmobile trail leading north under the power lines; this would take you in time to Blueberry Hill in Goshen. The route leading south along the shore of the lake is the Leicester Hollow Trail to Forest Dale. Either destination involves a considerable over-the-highway shuttle to return to your

16 Silver Lake

starting place. More likely you'll return the way you came, paying close attention to your snowplow and pole-dragging techniques. Remember that the last pitch is the steepest. Unless the snow is soft, you might do better to carry your skis at the end as at the beginning.

17 Frost Farm Loop

Around the loop: 4½ miles

Difficulty: moderate

Map: XC Middlebury

During Robert Frost's lifetime, cross-country skiing was "the road not taken," in contrast to the downhill variety that contributed so much to Vermont's winter economy. Now the equation is changing, and a marked touring trail can be found at the very edge of the farm where Frost did much of his later work. It begins at the Bread Loaf Campus of Middlebury College, but we approached it from the Robert Frost Wayside nearby and recommend that you do the same. However, you'll want a copy of the Middlebury trail map. Weekends and during holiday weeks, it can be obtained from the ski-touring center at Bread Loaf Campus, a cluster of yellow buildings on the north side of VT 125. At other times, visit the ticket desk in the base lodge at Middlebury College Snow Bowl, 2 miles farther on. Then return to the Frost Wayside to park your car; it's readily identified by a huge Forest Service sign on the south side of VT 125. A pull-through parking area with room for ten or twelve cars is located on the north side of the highway.

From the parking area, ski east for about 100 yards to an unplowed road with a power line alongside it. Follow this road north and uphill. The grade is easy to begin with

17 Frost Farm Loop

and gradually becomes more robust, though never too steep for well-waxed skis. It leads in about ½ mile to the boxy white clapboard farmhouse which Robert Frost owned from 1948 until his death in 1961, but which still goes by the name of its previous owner, Homer Noble. The road continues straight ahead and uphill, passing to the right of the farmhouse and a log cabin where Frost actually lived and wrote for most of the time he was in residence here.

Now a woods road, the trail passes through a plantation of red pine, finally leveling off and even descending a bit before entering the hardwoods about 1 mile from the

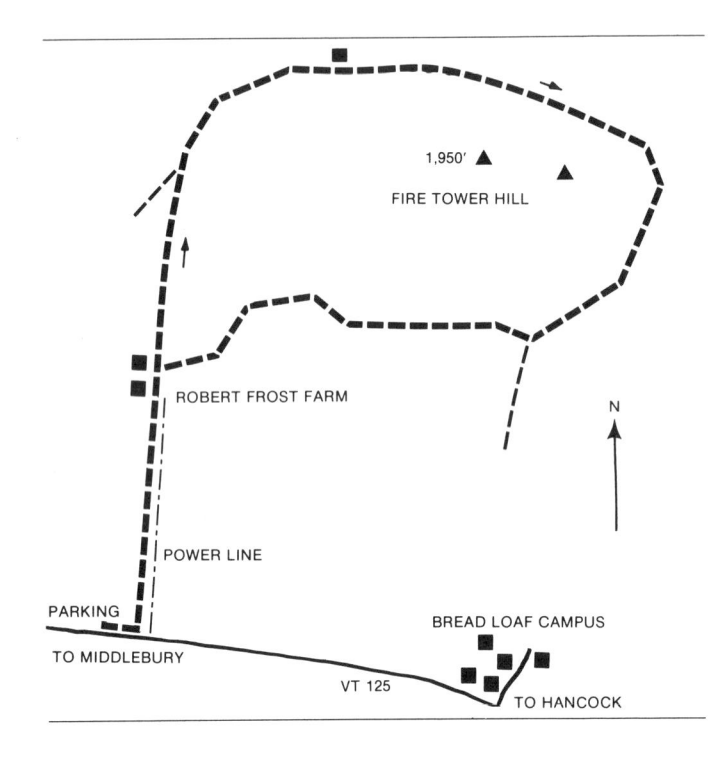

17 Frost Farm Loop

start. Here a hiking trail (often skied) comes in from the left, and the marked ski trail turns to the right. Look for a red rectangle. Following an eroded path that in the winter resembles a stream bed, the trail bears around to the right (east) and slabs the north side of Fire Tower Hill, climbing from time to time. About 1½ miles from the start, you'll come out in a clearing where stand several old apple trees and a dilapidated cottage known as the Blue Bed House. (Because, as a guesthouse on the estate of Joseph Battell, it once had a blue bed. Mr. Battell willed the Bread Loaf Inn and several thousand acres to Middlebury College, and this ski trail is one of the happy results of his philanthropy.) There are fine views of the mountains to the north and east, including Bread Loaf and Battell.

After leaving the clearing, the trail dips downhill—rather steeply at times—crosses a brook and bears around to the south, first uphill, then down. It skirts a fine hemlock grove and then turns west. Soon after this turning (about 2¾ miles from the start) the trail to Bread Loaf Campus leaves on the left. Turn right, toward Fire Tower Hill visible through the trees. When we skied this way, this leg was not well marked, or possibly some wayward soul had taken a wrong turning and the rest of us had doggedly followed him. Eventually, however, it all came together at a blue streamer, and we slabbed the south side of Fire Tower Hill as earlier we had slabbed the north.

At last the trail joins a woods road which it follows on a crooked but mostly downhill path. The going is fast at times through the evergreens, until the ski trail emerges

17 Frost Farm Loop

from the woods in a field with the Robert Frost cabin in view ahead, 4 miles from the start. Ski downhill to the farmhouse and return to the highway as you came—a beautiful run to finish the day.

The Robert Frost farm is an easy half-mile from the highway

18 Texas Falls

Distance: 1–6 miles

Difficulty: slight

Map: USGS Bread Loaf

Why Vermonters would name a settlement after the state of Texas, we can't imagine, unless they were longing for a hot sun and an open range. (A more prosaic explanation is that one of the hill farmers kept a herd of longhorn cattle.) The settlement has long since vanished, but the name remains on the topographical sheet in the form of Texas Falls and Texas Gap. Who could resist such an invitation? Not us, and on a cold February morning we skied up the access road to the icebound falls. As it turned out, we were the vanguard of twenty or more skiers, snowshoers, and even pedestrians who felt the lure of the falls that Sunday morning. And although we met no snowmobiles, their tracks were evident on the snow and in a Forest Service sign directing foot traffic to the left and machines to the right. A divided highway for winter travelers!

The access road to Texas Falls Recreation Area is on the north side of VT 125, about 3 miles west of Hancock (the junction of VT 100 and 125). There's a Forest Service sign opposite the entrance, and the highway is plowed wide enough at this point for four or five cars to park parallel to the travel lane, just before the access road and on the same side of the highway. You may find that the

18   Texas Falls

access road has been plowed. If the pavement is bare, you can drive up to a turnaround near the falls. But if there's snow on the roadway and your car doesn't have backcountry traction, you'll do better to park on VT 125 and ski the entire distance. The access road climbs at a very easy grade for about ½ mile, passing a few summer cottages in the process. Just before the turnaround, the falls are indicated by a Forest Service sign on your right (the sign may be buried in snow). The river itself is not visible from the road, so look and listen for the falls. A summer boardwalk leads down to the most picturesque section, where the Hancock Branch of the White River rumbles beneath the ice like traffic on a distant expressway. The stream has cut a considerable raceway out of the stone, and below the footbridge has made some fantastic sculpture among the rocks. Neither the bridge nor the boardwalk should be attempted on skis. You'll be much safer on foot, with a ski pole for balance—but be careful anyhow. One of the locals told us that somebody tumbles into the Hancock Branch almost every winter.

North of Texas Falls, the access road continues at the same easy grade to a picnic area, about 1 mile from the highway. Here public access is restricted by a gate, which is left open for winter travelers. In a few hundred yards the trail divides, with snowmobiles restricted to the right fork: a woods road to Texas Gap (about 4 miles from VT 125), thence to Forest Road 55 (about 5½ miles) and eventually to VT 100 at Granville (about 8 miles). Skiers do travel to Texas Gap, but it is a long, rough trail and should be attempted only by a strong party equipped for backwoods travel. When we went this way, skiing was made even more difficult by a missing bridge about ¼ mile north of the trail junction. See the Bread Loaf and Hancock topographical sheets for details of this trip.

In winter, Texas Falls is best admired from a distance ▶

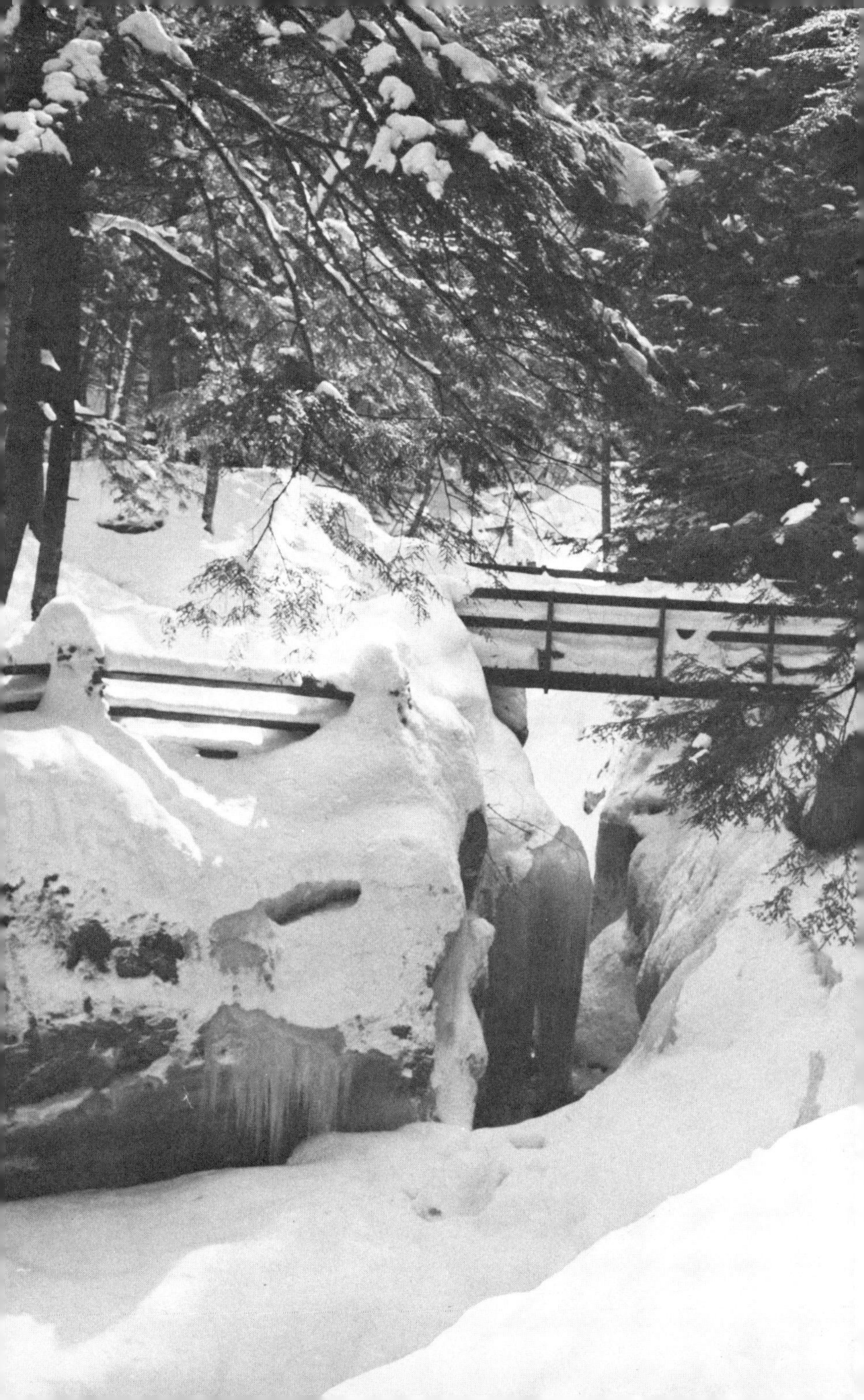

18 Texas Falls

Much more congenial is the left fork, which follows the Hancock Branch northwest to a point about 3 miles from the highway. The Forest Service rangers occasionally groom this trail with a homemade track-setter. This trip is suitable for intermediate skiers, and most of it can be negotiated by a sturdy novice; it ends, after three crossings of the Hancock Branch, at an unbridged section of the stream. The vertical rise is about 200 feet from the highway to the trail junction, and about 400 feet more from the junction to the end of the trail. Most of that comes in the final mile.

It's an enjoyable ride back to the highway—but beware. Even when the access road is six inches deep in snow, some people four-wheel it to the turnaround rather than ski the ½ mile from VT 125. It's rather disconcerting to meet a jeep in the ski track.

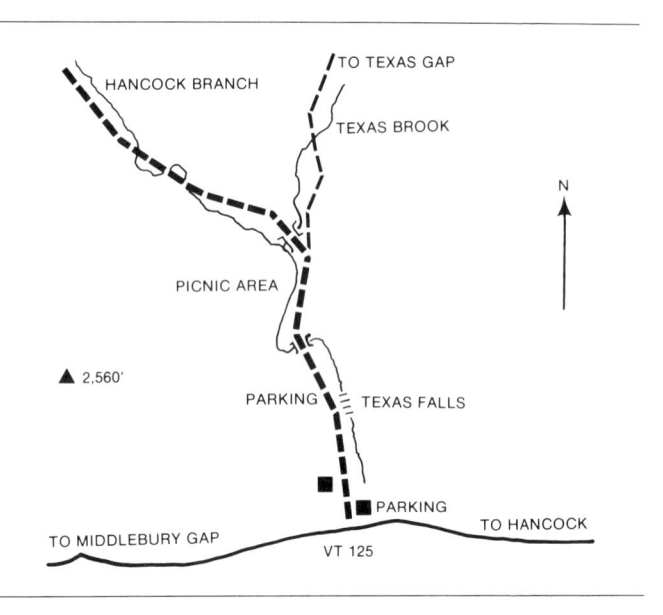

19 Cram Hill Loop

Around the
loop: 10 miles

Difficulty:
considerable

Map: USGS
Randolph

Find some friends you can trust, get an early start, and enjoy a Vermont adventure no motorist has ever experienced. We almost omitted this classic route because it wasn't *near anything,* and we've tried to cluster our tours for your convenience. We made an exception in this case. Cram Hill is a difficult loop, involving more than a mile of plowed road to hike, a grand total of 1,700 vertical feet to climb, and some chilling downhill runs—but ah! No trail this side of the Rockies ever satisfied us more. Approach from VT 12, between Randolph and Northfield (i.e., between Exit 4 and Exit 5 on Interstate 89). A cemetery signals the turn to West Brookfield, less than a mile west of the state highway. The village consists of a few houses, a church, and an old schoolhouse with the smallest belltower imaginable. There's usually room for a few cars to park beside the church. (Because of the limited parking, and because this is a major snowmobile route, it's best to schedule Cram Hill for a weekday.)

Ski south on an unplowed road, a sharp left turn just beyond the church and a shingled house. The road climbs steeply for about ½ mile, then levels off at a well-groomed farmstead which has been plowed out from the

Cram Hill Loop

south. Walk or ski alongside the road for a few hundred yards, then turn right (west) on an unplowed road which again takes you steeply uphill. Cold Brook is nearby on your left, open fields are on your right, and the no-trespassing signs are abundant. You'll soon reach a wrecked house with a beautiful view of the farmland to the east. Then you'll pass through a gate and into the hardwoods, where the road now looks more like a cart track. About 1¾ miles from the start, it takes you close to a cottage in a field, through which you'll have to look for the bordering trees that show where the road is located. The route is due west, and the road reenters the woods close to Cold Brook. Then you'll cross the brook (the road itself resembles a brookbed at times) and reach the height-of-land on this leg of your journey, about 800 vertical feet above West Brookfield.

The road now takes you steeply downhill through open woods, with Thresher Hill visible on your left. A snowmo-

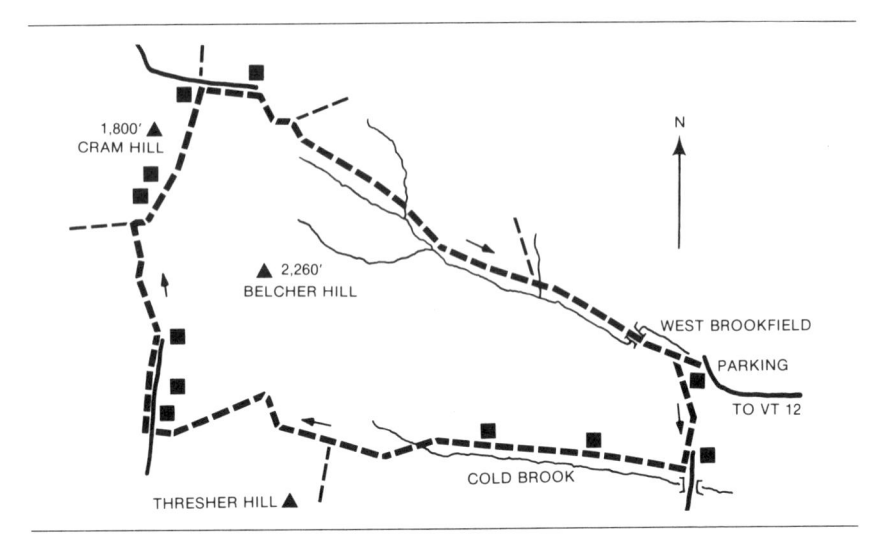

19   Cram Hill Loop

bile trail comes in from the left; then you pass a hunter's shack with a gorgeous view of the Northfield Mountains to the west. You have left pastoral Vermont behind you. The ramparts ahead are the."third range" of the Green Mountains, with the taller central peaks occasionally visible behind them. The road takes you down to a red house, about 4 miles from the start. Turn right (north) along a plowed road, leading uphill past a yellow house. We hiked it, but there was evidence that other skiers had chosen to traverse the fields to the west. In any event, the plowed road ends at another red house with a flagpole and many outbuildings. Ski straight ahead on the unplowed portion. It leads downhill to a brook, where another road comes in from the left; then it jogs to the right and climbs past two dilapidated cottages, each with a million-dollar view. After the second of these you have just about reached the summit of Cram Hill. The road is distinctly rougher now. It leads downhill to another house and many junked automobiles, then emerges upon a crossroads about 6¼ miles from the start. Turn right (east) on the plowed road leading uphill.

The plowed section soon ends at a shack with a large antenna, more junked automobiles, and a blue schoolbus which has been used as a camp. From this field is your last and best view of the Green Mountains to the west. Most of your climbing is now behind you. After a brief ski you'll reach the height-of-land on the eastbound leg of your journey, about 1,980 feet above sea level and 900 feet above West Brookfield. From here on, quite literally, the trip is all downhill. The route is generally southeast, with a stream below you on the right; you'll follow this stream all the way back to your car, through what at times is a narrow gulf. You can't go astray, but you might have trouble with the downhill stretches if the snowmobiles have left a narrow track. Sometimes we found it ad-

19 Cram Hill Loop

19 Cram Hill Loop

Near the height-of-land on the Cram Hill Loop

19   Cram Hill Loop

visable to ski off into the woods, then back to the trail again, making a long zigzag of the descent. In time, however, the trail becomes nearly level, then drops down to a shack where another road comes in from the left. You now pass an open area, recently timbered off, and the cottages become more numerous. This is the signal that you are coming down upon West Brookfield and the end of an arduous but memorable tour.

Caution: because of the many intersections along the route, each with the possibility of leading you astray, do not attempt this tour without a compass and a marked copy of the USGS Randolph sheet.

20 Austin Brook

To brook and return: 5 miles

Difficulty: moderate

Map: USGS Warren

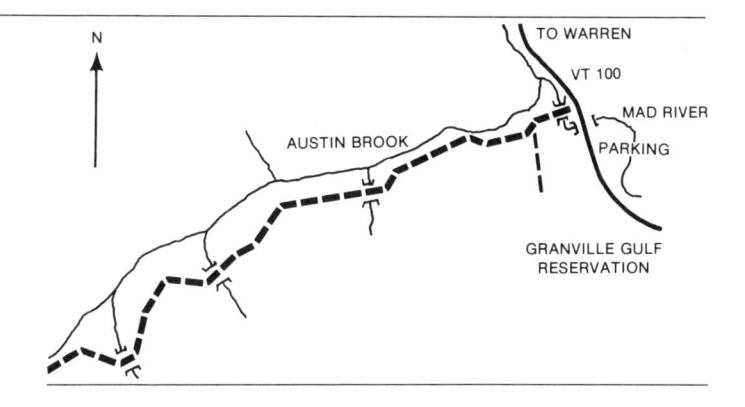

Some of the finest backcountry touring is to be found on unplowed roads, a fact that is rarely mentioned in ski-touring guides. Perhaps the people who cut trails and write about them are bushwhackers at heart and believe that following a road is somehow dishonest. However that may be, we're very fond of unplowed roads. Indeed, while we were fording streams and side-stepping hills on the Utley Brook Trail, we sometimes wondered why we were off in the woods when the clever snowmobilers had a clear and parallel route nearby. Of course, that's the problem with most such routes: they have become raceways for the snow machines. An exception is the Austin Brook Road, which the Forest Service has set aside for the exclusive use of skiers and snowshoers. It's even groomed from time to time. Best of all, there's a plowed parking area nearby—a rarity in Vermont, once you leave the established ski-touring centers. Accordingly, this is an excellent introduction to backcountry skiing. We've graded it "moderate" because some of the pitches are fairly steep, but a sturdy novice should have no trouble if the snow conditions are favorable.

Austin Brook flows into the Mad River just north of its source in Granville Gulf—what in neighboring New Hampshire would be called a "notch." More than a thousand acres in Granville Gulf have been set aside as a

Knee-deep powder on the Austin Brook Road

wilderness reserve by the state of Vermont. VT 100 passes through it. The parking lot for Austin Brook Road is located on the east side of the highway, exactly at the Granville-Warren town line and not far from the sign which marks the northern boundary of the state reservation. There's room for perhaps six automobiles. Leaving your car here, walk north about 100 yards and cross Mad River on the highway bridge. Then put on your skis, climb the snowbank, and cross the river a second time on the bridge that leads off to the left (west).

Austin Brook

The Austin Brook Road takes you briefly uphill, then levels off at a Green Mountain National Forest sign, where the road forks. (The lefthand road leads to an old timber sale and is missing at least one bridge; no repairs will be made because it enters a tract under consideration as the Bread Loaf Wilderness Area.) Keep to the right and climb an easy grade in a westerly direction. Austin Brook is on your right, distant at first but soon closing with the road and keeping you company as you climb more steeply and bear around to the left (southwest). This area is dominated by hardwoods, so that even without a specific overlook you can oftentimes see the landscape. A ridge is visible to the north: the other and steeper side of the valley formed by Austin Brook as it rushes down to join Mad River.

About ¾ mile from the start, the road levels off and crosses a tributary stream on a bridge. The view to the north is even finer here, as the opposing ridge becomes steeper and in places is literally walled with evergreens. After a hearty climb the road bears around to the left, levels off, and heads almost due south. Then it jogs westward, then south again, and crosses a second bridge about 1½ miles from the start. And so it goes: westward again on the level, then south as you climb nearly to the 1,900-foot contour, more than 600 feet above the highway. Finally the road drops down to the west, crosses a third bridge about 2¼ miles from the start, and loops around to its ending at Austin Brook itself. This crossing is not bridged, and unless you are prepared for wilderness travel you should stop right here. (This portion of the road, incidentally, is shown on the USGS Lincoln sheet.)

The return journey is considerably faster. Keep your speed under control, for the downhill runs can be exhilarating at times.

21 Ole's Loop

Around the
loop: 5 miles

Difficulty:
slight

Map: XC Ole's

Here's a gorgeous valley in the heart of the Green Mountains. It's as flat as a billiard table for the most part, with views through all arcs of the compass, and the sun shines upon it more days than not. That last fact is sworn to by local sailplane pilots, who explain that the prevailing winds over Lincoln Mountain create a "window" above the Sugarbush-Warren Airport even when surrounding towns are clouded in. Certainly the sun kept us company the entire time we were there. And we can report that something strange does happen to clouds in the vicinity of the airport: they look, well, *artificial,* as if they'd been shaped with a cookie cutter. The pilots call these clouds lenticulars, or "lennies" for short.

Ole Mosesen has taken advantage of these features—level terrain, wide vistas, and fair weather—to create a most unusual touring center. Unconnected either with an inn or a downhill ski resort, its headquarters are in the futuristic control tower of the Sugarbush-Warren Airport. To reach it, drive to Warren on VT 100. The village is off the highway to the east, and can be reached by either of two access roads; one of them has the advantage of passing through a covered bridge. Once in the center of town,

21 Ole's Loop

turn east on Brook Road (the sign says Roxbury) near the general store. Follow Brook Road for 2 miles, then turn left on Roxbury Gap Road, where there is a sign for the touring center. After ½ mile, turn right on Airport Road and follow it to the touring center parking lot. The shop is located downstairs in the airport building, and the sunburnt racer is Ole himself—pronounced "*oh*-lee," by the way. The trail fee at this writing is $1.50.

To ski the trail we have designated Ole's Loop, turn to your left (north) as you leave the airport building. The track runs between the road and the runway, then enters

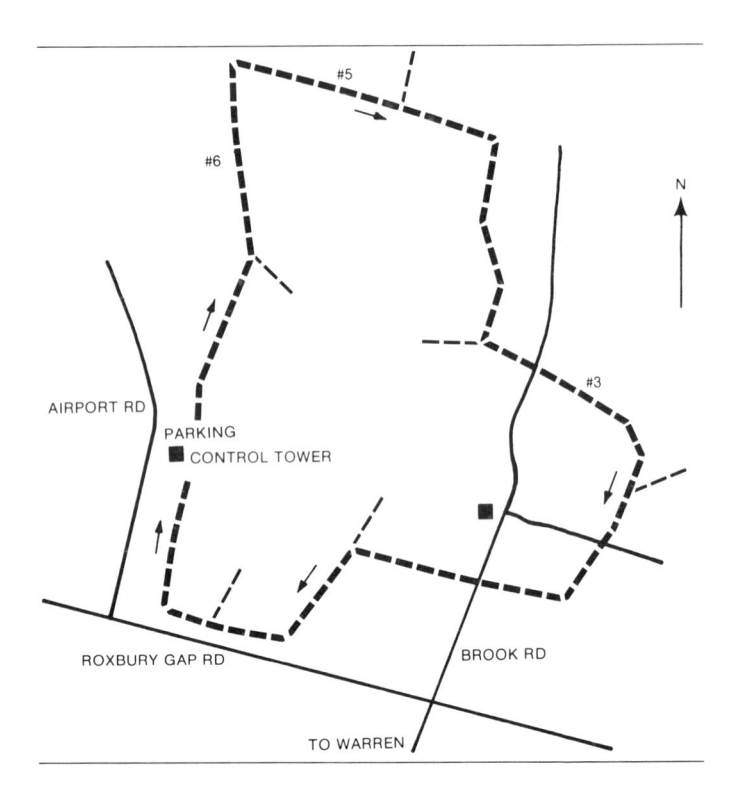

21 Ole's Loop

the woods and drops briskly downhill. Blue diamonds mark the route. Soon it brings you to a trail junction: bear left on #6. It crosses a brook, passed through a barbed-wire fence, and enters a fine stand of hemlock and fir. About 1 mile from the start, you emerge in a field with a breathtaking view of Lincoln Mountain to the west, with the downhill trails of Sugarbush etched upon it, while northwest you can see Mount Ellen and yet another network of trails. Keep to the east side of the field, then turn right (east) into a larger field with a view to the north. When we skied this way, trail #6 ended here and the continuation was marked #5. Crossing this second field, you again keep to the right for most of the distance, but jogging left (north) to pass through a fence. Out in the open, the trail is marked by blue diamonds on bamboo wands.

The farmsteads on Brook Road are visible ahead. Before reaching them, the trail swings to the right and takes you south along the road, crossing first a brook and then a driveway, and leading thus from field to field. About 2 miles from the start, it forks again. Turn left (west) on trail #3. (The right fork will take you back to the touring center if you'd rather not cross the road.) Take off your skis to negotiate the pavement, then put them on again to climb a hill to yet another trail junction. Bear right (south) from one field to the next, each with its own special view to south or west. At times you can see the airport building from which you began the tour, and if you're lucky the clouds may perform their cookie-cutter ritual for you. The lennies are a local phenomenon, caused by the same thermal updrafts that the sailplanes ride to higher altitudes.

At last the trail bears right and takes you downhill to Brook Road again, about 3½ miles from the start. After

21 Ole's Loop

Flat fields and fine clouds on Ole's Loop

21 Ole's Loop

recrossing the pavement, you'll come to a trail junction where you bear left (south) into the evergreen woods. It's a crooked path through the trees, but in time the trail takes you back into the open, skiing uphill and to the west, until you reach a final trail junction. Bear left once more, and in ½ mile you'll be back at the touring center.

22 Tucker Hill

To lodge and return: 10 miles

Difficulty: moderate

Map: XC Sugarbush Inn

The Sugarbush Inn and Tucker Hill Lodge joined forces a few years ago to cut one of the most exhilarating trails we've ever skied. It's not an expert run, exactly, but it's distinctly sporty when taken from south to north, and we recommend that you not attempt the journey until you've perfected your step-turn and snowplow techniques. With that caution, drive to the Sugarbush Inn Ski Touring Center. It's located on the south side of the Sugarbush ski area access road, about 2 miles west of VT 100 in Warren. The signs pointing to the downhill area are generous in size and number, and the touring center doesn't do badly in that department either. Recently it was taken over by the Rossignol ski company—proof, if any be needed, that touring has become a big business in Vermont. The trail fee at this writing is $2, including a sketch map of the trails. The one you're interested in is #5 on the local trail system.

To reach the trailhead, walk back to the access road and cross it. There's a small white house opposite the touring center; to the left of it you'll see a blue diamond trail marker on a telephone pole. You begin with a sharp downhill into the evergreens, followed by a climb. Then

Tucker Hill

the trail levels off and enters the hardwoods, drops downhill, meanders past a small beaver pond, and enters the evergreens again. Now you're skiing along a valley—a notch, almost—across an extended system of beaver ponds. A groomed trail leaves on the right; this is #5-A, taking skiers back to the touring center after a look

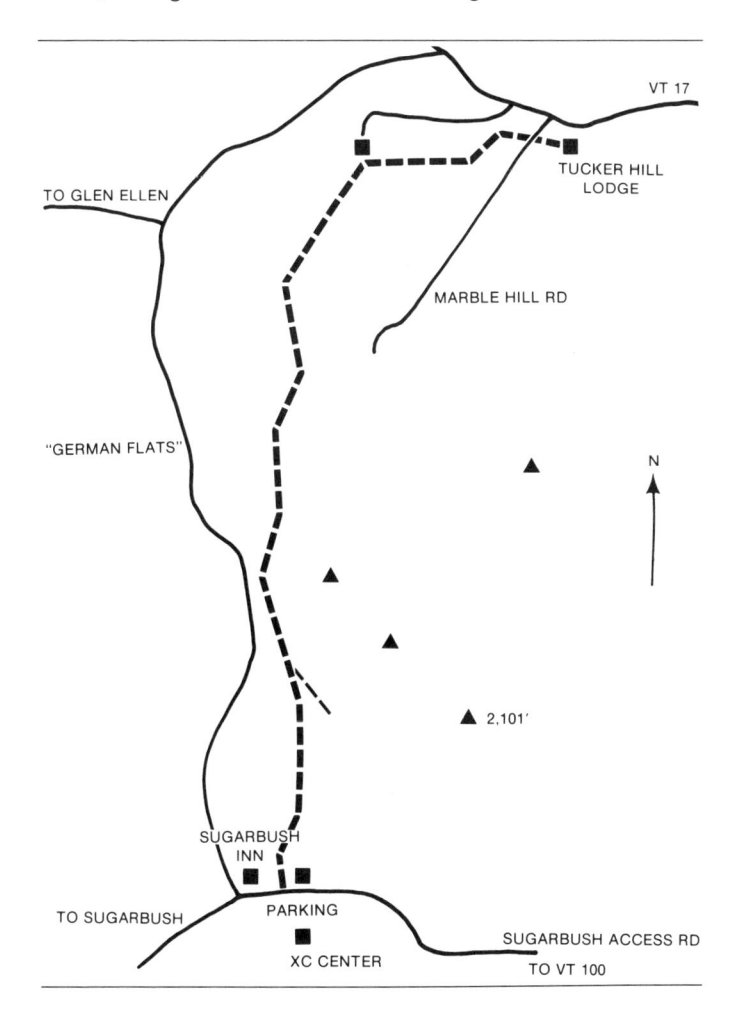

22 Tucker Hill

at the beaver works. For your part, ski straight down the valley, then climb a hardwood ridge with views of the trails on Mount Lincoln, otherwise known as Sugarbush. About 1 mile from the start, the trail swings so close to German Flats Road that you can hear the traffic; at this point you're in the backyard of an expensive second-home development.

We promised sporty skiing—now it begins. The trail goes wildly downhill on a crooked path, then climbs again. And so it goes, up and down. There are more views of ski trails to the west, this time upon the face of Mount Ellen. Your own personal downhill trail now takes a breather and even climbs for a bit into the evergreens. Don't be fooled: another wild career through the hardwoods is still to come. Finally, however, you'll reach a sign for Sugarhouse Loop, 4 miles from the start. The trail now joins a woods road and follows it for a time, but veers off to the right as it nears a white house. After passing through a cluster of gray birches, you'll come to another trail junction; bear left here into an incredible stand of white pines, reaching straight and clear to a canopy that must be one hundred feet above the forest floor. These trees were planted in 1912, and unfortunately the soil is too sandy to sustain them. Because windstorms bring them down in quantity, they are fated to be lumbered off.

Soon there's a final trail junction. Bear left again, dropping down to Marble Hill Road. Cross the pavement to Tucker Hill Lodge, a pretty place that looks more like a private home than an inn. On weekends or during holiday weeks, head for the main building and the tavern, where you can stoke the inner skier with soup and sandwiches, not to mention cider, beer, and wine. Weekdays, the soup pot is moved across to the touring center. Cider

A groomed track makes short work of the miles

is the most potent beverage then available, but the bill of fare is otherwise the same. A couple dollars should restore you for the 5-mile return journey to the Sugarbush Inn.

You can, of course, run the trail from north to south, and at this writing you'd save $.50 by doing so. You'd also put the uphill section in the first half of the trip, when you're fresher. (To reach Tucker Hill Lodge by road, follow VT 17 about 2 miles west from VT 100 at Irasville.) However, the staff at Tucker Hill was so agreeable—and the soup so hearty—that we suggest you take it the way we did. A more enjoyable lunch would be hard to imagine.

23 Bolton Lodge

To shelter and
return: 4 miles

Difficulty:
mostly slight

Map: XC
Bolton

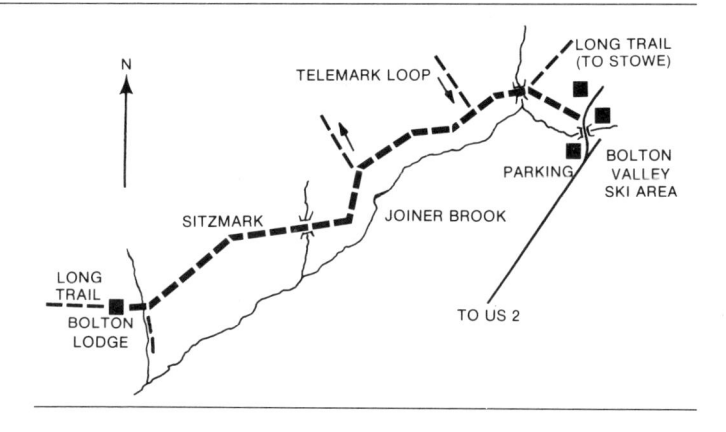

There's a confusion of nomenclature here. To a hiker on the Long Trail, Bolton Lodge is a stone and stucco shelter, one of many such buildings en route from the Massachusetts border to the Canada line. To the downhill skiers who occupied this valley more recently, Bolton Lodge is the place where they drink their hot chocolates between runs. Accordingly, the Long Trail building has been rechristened Bolton Valley Shelter on local maps. But a lodge it was when it was built in 1928—six years before there was such a thing as a downhill ski area in Vermont—and Bolton Lodge it shall remain for purposes of this tour.

23 Bolton Lodge

To begin, drive to the self-contained ski resort known as Bolton Valley, located off US 2 between exits 10 and 11 of Interstate 89. (Don't stay on the interstate: you can't get here from there.) Among its other amenities, the valley claims 35 miles of cross-country trails, but they aren't patrolled and may not be groomed. A map can be obtained at the registration desk or at the ticket window, located in the main building east of the parking lot—a hotel and base lodge in one. You also pay the trail fee ($2 at this writing) at the ticket window, or at the trailhead on busy days.

The route to Bolton Lodge is an old logging road that is now a link in the Long Trail. To reach it, walk straight ahead (due north) from the parking lot to a work road leading past the tennis courts and a residential complex. You can probably ski on the road or beside it. It leads downhill, past a small brown shack, then divides. Turn left on the unplowed portion, which bears signs identifying it as Trail #1, called the Sitzmark. This leads northwest about ¼ mile to Joiner Brook Junction, where you turn left (south) on the main trail. (The northern leg is the Long Trail to Mount Mansfield. It soon forks, with one branch doubling back to the downhill ski slopes and the other leading in 12 hardscrabble miles to the Trapp Family Lodge in Stowe. This is a wilderness trail and requires robust skiers and equipment.)

Southbound on the Sitzmark, you'll find the route marked both by the white paint blazes of the Long Trail and the yellow squares of the local touring system. Almost immediately, the Telemark Trail (#5) comes in from the right. From here on, for nearly 1 mile, the Sitzmark heads downhill through a forest of young hardwoods. Then it crosses a bridge. The southern leg of the Telemark Trail forks to the right, and a rather steep downhill pitch soon follows. The Sitzmark meanders for about ½ mile, crosses another bridge, and ends at a sudden turn to the left. Here the old logging road continues steeply downhill to join the Bolton Valley access road. To the right, across a brook, stands Bolton Lodge. The door is unlocked, and if snow hasn't sealed it off you're welcome to step inside or even to spend the night. The facilities are spartan: a sheet-metal stove, a plank table and benches, double-decker bunks with mattresses of board, and perhaps a candle stuck in a wine bottle. Beyond the lodge,

The trail to Bolton Lodge follows an old logging road

23 Bolton Lodge

the Long Trail leads southwest to Jonesville—far too rugged a path for skiing. Through the scattering hardwoods you command splendid views of Bolton Valley and (due south) Camel's Hump, the fourth highest mountain in Vermont.

Since the return journey is mostly uphill, it will be more strenuous than the outbound leg. If that's not challenge enough, you can vary the route by taking the Telemark Trail as shown on the sketch map. (The Telemark should only be skied in a clockwise direction.) This variant adds about 1 mile—and one whole degree of expertise—to the tour. It's a long climb to the northwest before the Telemark levels off and swings around to the east; even then there's more climbing to be done, and you reach the 2,300-foot contour before turning southward and dropping down toward the ski area. It's a steep drop at times, before ending at the Sitzmark just below Joiner Brook Junction.

24 Trapp Cabin Loop

Around the
loop: 8 miles

Difficulty:
moderate

Map: XC Trapp

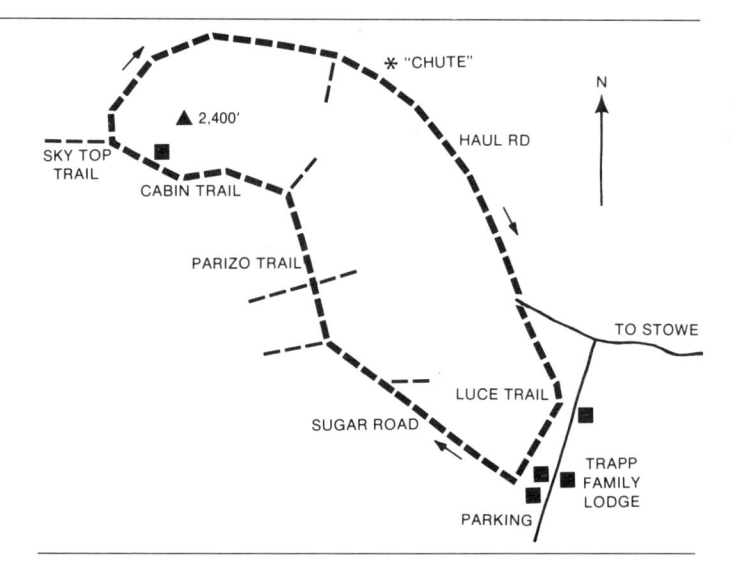

The Trapp Family Lodge maintains one of the oldest—and certainly one of the most elaborate—cross-country skiing facilities in the United States. The ski shop would do credit to a downhill resort, and there's $20,000 worth of grooming equipment to keep the trails in creampuff condition. If this sounds too sophisticated for a back-country skier, be assured that the Trapps have provided for you as well. High on the flank of Round Top mountain, a bit more than 3 miles from the touring center, there's a

24   Trapp Cabin Loop

The Trapp Cabin is a favorite destination for tour-skiers

log cabin where you can back up to a fire while enjoying hot chocolate, soup, or sandwiches. Taking the cabin as a way station on a circular tour makes for one of the classic ski routes in the Stowe area.

Stowe is everybody's favorite ski resort, located on VT 100 about 10 miles from Interstate 89 (Waterbury exit). For the touring center, as for the downhill ski areas, turn left at the traffic light in the village. This is VT 108, containing more motels and ski lodges than any other highway we've driven along. Turn left again 2 miles from the traffic light. The access road is 2¼ miles of uphill grind, with several hairpin turns, but with a sturdy heart and deep-cleated tires you will come in time to the Trapp Family Lodge, like a Bavarian wedding cake on the left side of the road. The touring center is just beyond, on the right, and just beyond that is a huge parking lot for skiers. Go into the touring center to pay your trail fee ($1 at this writing), to pick up a trail map ($1.50), and to marvel at how things are done in Stowe.

The Trapps ask two things of their guests, besides the normal skier courtesies: leave your dog at home, and please don't arrive at the cabin late in the afternoon. It closes at 3:30 p.m., more for your safety than for the convenience of the crew.

Take the Sugar Road directly behind the touring center, at the northern edge of a pasture which serves as a practice area. You'll roll along in pleasant style through a mixed evergreen and hardwood forest, an imperceptible downhill followed by an imperceptible uphill. Just under 1 mile from the touring center, the Telemark Trail comes in from the right. About ¼ mile beyond this junction, the Sugar Road ends at Picnic Knoll. This is a small field with fine views over the Miller Brook Valley. To here you have gained less than 100 vertical feet, but now the climb begins in earnest on the Parizo Trail—a divided ski-way, no less, with uphill and downhill sections required by the steepness of the pitch. (Otherwise the climbers would be in jeopardy from those descending.) In the next 1½ miles you'll gain 435 vertical feet, broken only once when you cross the Old County Road. At last the climb ends at three-way fork. Take the lefthand route—the Cabin Trail—and move along in fine style for a bit more than ½ mile to the building for which it was named. The cabin is a pleasant sight at the edge of Slayton Pasture. Built in 1971, the prefabricated log structure exists solely for the greater glory of backcountry touring. In the early years, parties could spend the night here; now it is occupied by a couple who serve up snacks, a

24   Trapp Cabin Loop

warm fire, and hospitality to all comers. Soup, a sandwich, and coffee could be had for about $3 when we passed through.

After leaving the cabin—which is likely to take a while—you have a choice of routes for the return. You can ski back whence you came, which is the quickest route but one which involves a tortuous amount of snowplowing on the Parizo Trail. Better yet, you can strike off westward on the Haul Road, at the other end of the field from where you arrived. The Haul Road shortly takes you to the Little Meadow, where the Sky Top Trail leaves on the left. (Sky Top is an 8-mile loop for expert skiers only: talk to the folks at the cabin before attempting this variant). The Haul Road now swings around to the north and descends about 400 vertical feet before the Oslo Trail comes in from the right. Following this junction is the Chute—the only really steep drop on this route. The trail descends to a plowed road, crosses it, and reaches the Trapp complex about 4¼ miles from the cabin. You then follow the Luce Trail about ½ mile back to the touring center.

25 Smuggler's Notch

To cave and
return: 4 miles

Difficulty:
slight

Map: USGS
Mt. Mansfield

Smuggler's Notch earned its name from the dark doings that occupied this area during the War of 1812. New England had no appetite for another war, so soon after the Revolution, and Yankee businessmen valued British goods more highly than such principles as freedom of the seas. Accordingly a brisk but illegal trade sprang up between Montreal and Boston. The smugglers chose this deep cleft in the mountains as their safest route past the U.S. revenue agents, and legend has it that they hid their contraband in a cave at the height-of-land. However that may be, the cave is a splendid destination for a ski tour, and even as a picnic spot in mild weather. The Smuggler's Notch tour is best scheduled after a recent snowfall. The wind blows hard through this north-south gap between Mount Mansfield and Spruce Peak, and the route is open to snowmobiles. Between them, they can produce a miserable surface for skiing after a few weeks without snow.

The notch road is VT 108 between Stowe and Jeffersonville. It can be skied from either side, but there are more skiers on the south, so that's the way we approached it. Leave Stowe village as described in the previous tour.

25   Smuggler's Notch

About 8 miles from the traffic light, and just beyond the access road to Spruce Peak ski area, the pavement ends at a spot plowed wide enough for a few dozen automobiles. Winter climbers are the people most likely to park here. Follow their snowshoe tracks over the snowbank straight ahead, and you will find yourself skiing up a gentle rise. Soon there is a magnificent view of the notch, with beetling cliffs on the right (east) side. A section of these will gradually take shape as the Elephant's Head, a rock formation that actually looks more like a monkey than a pachyderm.

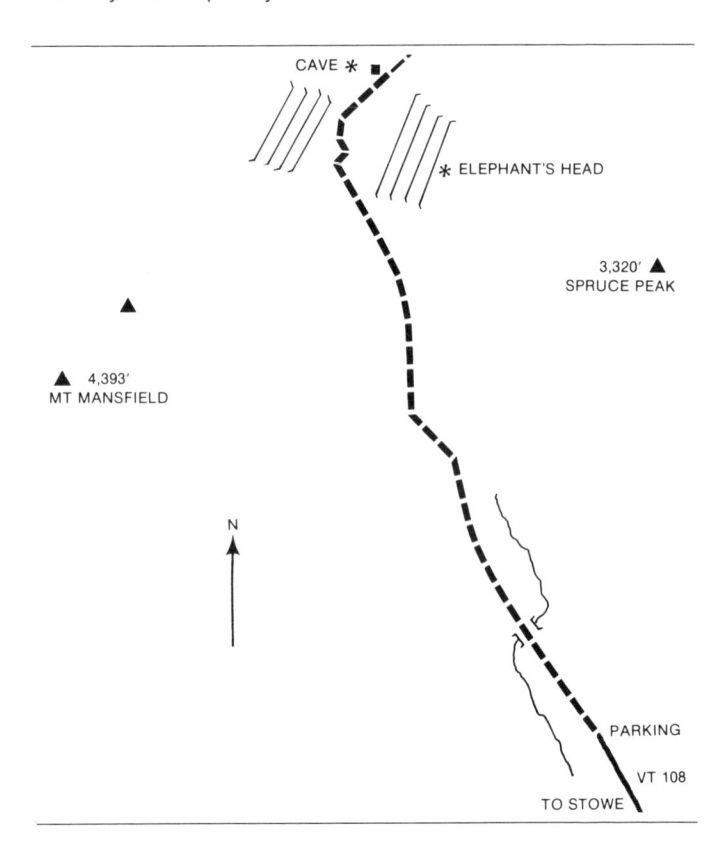

25 Smuggler's Notch

About ⅓ mile from the start, the Long Trail comes in from the left. This is where most of the winter climbers are bound; a few yards in from the road, there is a signboard advising them of the most recent conditions on Mount Mansfield. (The Long Trail coincides with the road from here to the height-of-land.) Not long after, you'll pass a picnic area on the right, then a bridge which marks the boundary between the townships of Stowe and Cambridge. There is a standard highway marker here, and others ahead, giving you the queer feeling that at any moment you might be overtaken by a laundry truck or a carload of tourists.

The road now climbs more steeply, though never so steep that a well-waxed pair of skis can't manage the grade. Finally VT 108 begins to wind between huge boulders. The snow is likely to be sculpted here, and in places the wind may have scoured it down to ice. Pick your way with caution, but don't fear that another boulder will tumble down from Mount Mansfield or Spruce Peak. They've been here for centuries, as is evidenced by the trees that have taken root in the dirt and debris on top of them. Ski between these boulders until you reach a state park building resembling a lean-to shelter, but made of cut stone. This is the height-of-land, 2 miles from where you left your car. Directly to the right (east) you'll see the white paint blazes of the Long Trail, heading up Spruce Peak. Directly to the left (west) is the Smuggler's Cave, slightly uphill from the stone building. It's not a sure-enough hole in the mountain, but rather a passageway formed by the great boulders as they tumbled upon one another. Though sheltered from the wind, the cave can be a grim place, especially when its walls are rimed with frost. If you don't find it congenial, you can return to the roadway and entertain yourself by looking for the Smuggler's Face, a rock formation high on the cliff to the west.

25 Smuggler's Notch

"Smuggler's Cave"—where contraband may have been stored

25 Smuggler's Notch

Strong skiers may wish to continue north along VT 108 to the Madonna Mountain ski area. This leg of the notch road is gentle, but it does double the distance to be skied, with an additional uphill on the return. If that seems too ambitious, just ski south again to your car—a lovely downhill run, provided there is a bit of soft snow to brake you on the turns.

Sally and Daniel Ford

Also by Daniel Ford

The Country Northward
A Hiker's Journal on the Trail in the White Mountains of New Hampshire

"Lively, entertaining—really an excellent piece of work."—*Yankee*

With Sally Ford

25 Ski Tours in the White Mountains
A Cross-Country Skier's Guide to New Hampshire's Backcountry Trails

"Some books originate at the drawing board, while others are born out of love of the out-of-doors in winter. This is a guide written by people who have been there!"—*Nordic Skiing*

"Anyone interested in cross-country skiing in the White Mountains should get a copy of this book. It'll save time, offer tours you haven't heard of, and give you some fun merely planning your next excursion."—*New Hampshire Times*